WILLIAMS-SONOMA

The Best of
THANKSGIVING

weldon**owen**

Contents

Time for Thanks

Although we all gather around a table to give thanks on the fourth Thursday in November, there's really no single way to celebrate Thanksgiving. That's why we've put together this abundant collection of Thanksgiving recipes that help you blend inspired new dishes with your most dearly held traditions. In these pages, you'll find more than 80 recipes for cocktails and appetizers; main dishes, including six imaginative ways to cook turkey, plus a glazed ham and a tempting vegetarian potpie; stuffings and breads; twenty sides of all kinds; gravies and relishes; holiday-themed desserts, including the iconic pies (pumpkin, apple, and pecan) and other tempting sweets; and four standout sandwiches for making the most of the leftovers.

Most of the work of Thanksgiving, as with any kind of entertaining, should be done in advance of the event itself. With a good plan in hand, you will be able to join the party and share in the fun. Look for useful tips about creating a realistic timeline for a stress-free meal on pages 8–9, pointers on setting the scene on pages 11–12, ideas for pairing wine with your meal on page 99, tips and tricks for roasting and serving a beautiful bird on pages 100–104, and recipes for staples such as stock and pie dough on pages 106–107.

With this book in your arsenal, you'll have everything you need for a wonderful holiday meal. But remember, cooking what you love and serving your feast with joy are key to giving your family and friends something to be truly thankful for: a celebration to remember.

Timeline

The key to stress-free entertaining is to plan ahead—especially when it comes to the Thanksgiving meal. This timeline will help you stay on track. You can do much of the prep work beforehand, so you'll have plenty of time to enjoy the company of your family and friends on the day of the feast.

1 TO 2 WEEKS BEFORE THANKSGIVING

- Confirm the number of guests and plan the menu
- Order the turkey
- Plan the table setting, serving dishes, and decorations
- Read through all your recipes to determine the food and cooking tools you will need
- Make the shopping and to-do lists

A FEW DAYS BEFORE THANKSGIVING

o Prepare the turkey brine (if using) but do not add the turkey; cover and refrigerate

o Prepare any food that can be made a few days ahead of time, such as pie dough and cranberry sauce

THE DAY BEFORE THANKSGIVING

o Complete the food shopping

o If you ordered a fresh turkey, pick it up or have it delivered

o If you are brining the turkey, place it in the brine and refrigerate

o Prepare dishes that can be made in advance, such as soup and pie

o Chop vegetables for side dishes; refrigerate them in covered bowls or zippered plastic bags

o Peel and cut the potatoes; place in cold water and refrigerate

o Set the table

THE DAY OF THANKSGIVING

o Refrigerate wines that need chilling, or place on ice in a cooler if you need refrigerator space

o **Prepare the stuffing and other side dishes**

o Prepare the turkey for roasting and put in the oven at the determined time. If you plan to stuff the bird, do not stuff it until just before you put it in the oven

o While the turkey is resting, make the gravy and cook or reheat the side dishes

o Arrange the dishes on a buffet or the dining table

o Carve the turkey and serve your guests

Setting the Scene

Whether your celebration will be formal or casual, it's a good idea to plan ahead of time how to set up and decorate your space.

Begin by choosing a color palette that looks good with your tableware and the room. That palette will help you create a centerpiece, place settings, and room decorations that will work together to set a festive mood. Stick with two or three colors and a few complementary textures, such as wood, pewter, and foliage. The key is restraint and simplicity.

Also, think about how you want to serve your food, whether it's arranged on an elegant buffet or offered more casually from an open kitchen. A rolling kitchen cart or folding table can stand in for a buffet in a pinch, but make the effort to ensure it looks inviting by lining it with a tablecloth or runner that coordinates with your color theme.

Taking the time to think about the ambience in advance will ease stress on the day of the meal. Turn the page for more ideas on organizing and making your house look beautiful for the upcoming feast.

Planning for the Feast

To set a celebratory mood and help ease any stress on Thanksgiving Day, take time to think about the details of your meal in advance.

○ **Choose a Spot** The first step is to determine where the feast will be held. If your dining room table cannot accommodate your crowd, borrow additional tables or chairs from friends or rent them from an event rental company.

○ **Check Your Supplies** Check all your linens, glassware, tableware, and flatware well before the party to make sure you have everything you need. Purchase, borrow, or rent any items that are missing.

○ **Plan Your Serving Pieces** The day before the event, set out all your serving pieces—carving board, serving platters, serving dishes, and the like—on your buffet or table. Write the name of each menu item on a sticky note or piece of tape and attach it to the appropriate serving platter or dish to remind you of which food goes on each piece. When purchasing new serveware, choose neutral or white pieces. That makes it easy to add to your collection over time and ensures the food takes center stage.

○ **Select the Utensils** Set out the appropriate serving utensils for each item on your menu—such as a fork for the turkey, large spoons or elegant tongs for the side dishes, and a pie server for dessert—so you won't need to hunt for them at the last minute. Borrow, rent, or purchase items that are missing.

○ **Add a Centerpiece** To make the table look special, select an attractive centerpiece that evokes a holiday theme and creates a focal point for the room. It can be anything from a floral arrangement with autumnal blooms or an heirloom bowl filled with seasonal fruits or vegetables to a slender vase of olive branches or fall berries on the stem. Keep the centerpiece natural and uncomplicated, and avoid too many tall or wide elements that could block sight lines at the table.

○ **Bring in the Outdoors** Visit your local farmers' market and gather a selection of seasonal fruits, such as persimmons, pomegranates, pears, and quinces. Arrange the fruits in low wooden or ceramic bowls and set them around the room to add a seasonal ambience to your house.

○ **Delight in the Details** Matching place cards in holders, charming salt and pepper shakers, and complementary napkin rings will all help contribute to a streamlined style. If you will be hosting the Thanksgiving meal every year, invest in tabletop elements that can be reused.

○ **Set up a Drinks Bar** Designate an area—a side table or a free countertop—where you can arrange the drinks. Set out glasses, ice, and assorted beverages for family and friends to help themselves.

○ **Light the Room** Use floor lamps, table lamps, and groupings of large candles to create soft, flattering pools of light. Or, create a welcoming glow with tall taper candles placed in elegant silver holders. Mix and match heights but use coordinated candles to create an effortlessly elegant arrangement. Dim or turn off overhead lights.

○ **Add a Special Touch** Thanksgiving celebrations offer the perfect opportunity to add an extra flourish to individual place settings. This could be a little bundle of fragrant herbs or small, lightly scented flowers or a homemade gift that guests can take with them to remind them of the meal.

Drinks & Appetizers

Maple-Bourbon Smash 19

Pomegranate Gin Fizz 19

Sparkling Apple Punch 19

Virgin Cosmopolitan 19

Crostini with Pear Chutney 20

Mushroom Turnovers 20

Arugula Salad with Goat Cheese & Pecans 23

Watercress, Endive & Apple Salad 23

Butternut Squash Soup 24

Shrimp Bisque 24

Cream of Chestnut Soup 25

Carrot Soup with Orange & Ginger 25

Maple-Bourbon Smash

PREP TIME 2 MINUTES **SERVES** 1

Ice cubes

¼ cup (2 fl oz/60 ml) bourbon

2 tablespoons maple syrup

2 tablespoons fresh lemon juice

Lemon twist for garnish

Fill a cocktail shaker with ice. Pour the bourbon, maple syrup, and lemon juice into the shaker. Stir until thoroughly chilled, about 20 seconds. Strain the mixture into a double old-fashioned glass filled with ice cubes. Garnish with the lemon twist and serve.

Pomegranate Gin Fizz

PREP TIME 2 MINUTES **SERVES** 1

Crushed ice

¼ cup (2 fl oz/60 ml) gin

½ cup (4 fl oz/125 ml) pomegranate juice

1 tablespoon Grand Marnier

Chilled club soda

Lime wedge

Pomegranate seeds for garnish

Fill a highball glass with crushed ice. Pour the gin, pomegranate juice, and Grand Marnier over the ice. Top with a splash of club soda and stir gently. Squeeze the lime wedge over the top. Garnish with the pomegranate seeds and serve.

Sparkling Apple Punch

PREP TIME 2 MINUTES **SERVES** 1

½ cup (4 fl oz/125 ml) chilled sparkling wine

1–2 tablespoons Calvados

Very thin apple slices for garnish

White currants for garnish (optional)

Pour the sparkling wine into a Champagne flute or coupe. Add the Calvados. Garnish with 1 or 2 apple slices and a small cluster of currants, if using, and serve.

Virgin Cosmopolitan

PREP TIME 2 MINUTES **SERVES** 1

Ice cubes

¼ cup (2 fl oz/60 ml) sweetened cranberry juice

¼ cup (2 fl oz/60 ml) fresh tangerine juice

1 tablespoon fresh lime juice

Lime twist for garnish

Put a martini glass in the freezer to chill for at least 30 minutes. Just before serving, fill a cocktail shaker half full with ice. Pour in the cranberry juice, tangerine juice, and lime juice. Cover with the lid and shake vigorously up and down until very cold, about 10 seconds. Strain the mixture into the chilled glass. Garnish with the lime twist and serve.

Crostini with Pear Chutney

PREP TIME 25 MINUTES   **COOK TIME** 35 MINUTES
MAKES ABOUT 24 CROSTINI

FOR THE CHUTNEY
1 lemon
1 orange
1 fresh rosemary sprig
1 bay leaf
1 cinnamon stick
1 tablespoon unsalted butter
2 shallots, finely chopped
2 lb (1 kg) pears, peeled, cored, and finely diced

¼ cup (2 fl oz/60 ml) pear brandy or cognac
⅓ cup (2½ oz/75 g) firmly packed golden brown sugar

Arugula leaves
Toasted baguette slices
Aged goat cheese, thinly sliced

To make the chutney, using a vegetable peeler, remove the zest of the lemon and orange in wide strips. Squeeze the juice from the lemon and orange and set them aside separately. Tie the zest, rosemary, bay leaf, and cinnamon stick in a square of cheesecloth to make a sachet.

In a saucepan over medium-high heat, melt the butter. Add the shallots and pears and sauté until the pears begin to release their juices, 6–8 minutes. Deglaze the pan with the brandy, stirring well with a wooden spoon, and simmer until the liquid is reduced by one-third, 2–3 minutes.

Add the brown sugar, ½ cup (4 fl oz/125 ml) orange juice, 2 tablespoons lemon juice, and the herb-spice sachet. (Reserve any remaining juice for another use.) Bring the liquid to a simmer, then reduce the heat to medium-low and cook until the liquid has nearly evaporated, about 25 minutes. Remove and discard the sachet and let the chutney cool.

To assemble the crostini, place a few arugula leaves on each baguette slice and top with 1 or 2 thin slices of cheese. Top each with a dollop of chutney and arrange on a platter.

Mushroom Turnovers

PREP TIME 45 MINUTES   **INACTIVE PREP TIME** 2 HOURS
COOK TIME 30 MINUTES   **MAKES** 20–24 TURNOVERS

2 tablespoons unsalted butter
2 tablespoons olive oil
3 tablespoons finely chopped shallot
¾ lb (375 g) cremini mushrooms, brushed clean and finely chopped
1½ teaspoons chopped fresh thyme
1½ teaspoons chopped fresh rosemary

Kosher salt and freshly ground pepper
½ cup (4 fl oz/125 ml) heavy cream
¼ cup (1 oz/30 g) finely shredded Gruyère cheese
1 recipe Basic Pie Dough for a double-crust pie (page 107), shaped into 2 disks and chilled
1 egg, lightly beaten with 1 tablespoon water

In a sauté pan over medium-high heat, melt the butter with the oil. Add the shallot and sauté until softened but not browned, about 2 minutes. Add the mushrooms, thyme, and rosemary, and season with salt and pepper. Sauté until the mushrooms are tender and the liquid is almost evaporated, 10–12 minutes. Raise the heat to high and add the cream. Cook, stirring often, until the mixture comes to a boil, 2–3 minutes, then remove from the heat and let cool completely. Stir in the cheese.

Preheat the oven to 400°F (200°C). Line 2 baking sheets with parchment paper.

Remove 1 dough disk from the refrigerator and let stand for 5 minutes. On a lightly floured work surface, roll out the dough into a large rectangle about ⅛ inch (3 mm) thick. Cut the dough into 3½-inch (9-cm) squares, rerolling the scraps as needed to yield at least 10 squares.

Place a scant 1 tablespoon of the cooled filling (do not overfill) in the center of each pastry square, then lightly brush the edges with the egg wash. Fold the pastry in half to cover the filling, forming a triangle. Using the tines of a fork, crimp the edges to seal. As each pastry is completed, transfer to a prepared baking sheet and refrigerate to keep cool. Repeat with the remaining dough disk and filling.

Brush the tops of the pastries with the remaining egg wash. Bake until golden, 15–20 minutes. Let cool slightly before serving.

Arugula Salad with Goat Cheese & Pecans

PREP TIME 15 MINUTES   **SERVES** 8–10

¾ cup (3 oz/90 g) dried cranberries

1½ cups (12 fl oz/375 ml) boiling water

3 tablespoons fresh orange juice

1½ tablespoons cider vinegar

1½ teaspoons Dijon mustard

6 tablespoons (3 fl oz/90 ml) canola oil

3 tablespoons chopped fresh flat-leaf parsley

Kosher salt and freshly ground pepper

10 oz (315 g) baby arugula

1¼ cups (5 oz/155 g) pecan halves, toasted

5 oz (155 g) fresh goat cheese, crumbled

Toast pecans!

Put the dried cranberries in a small heatproof bowl and pour the boiling water over them. Let steep for 10 minutes, then drain.

In another small bowl, whisk together the orange juice, vinegar, and mustard. Slowly whisk in the oil. Fold in the soaked cranberries and parsley to make a vinaigrette. Season to taste with salt and pepper. (You can make the vinaigrette up to 2 days ahead of time and refrigerate it in an airtight container. Let the vinaigrette stand at room temperature for 20 minutes before assembling the salad.)

To serve, put the arugula in a large bowl, drizzle with the vinaigrette to taste (you may not need all of it), and toss well. Scatter the pecans and cheese over the top and serve right away.

Watercress, Endive & Apple Salad

PREP TIME 25 MINUTES   **SERVES** 8–10

⅔ cup (3¾ oz/110 g) hazelnuts

3 large bunches watercress, about 1½ lb (750 g) total weight, tough stems removed

3 heads Belgian endive, about 1 lb (500 g) total weight, cored and separated into leaves

⅓ cup (3 fl oz/80 ml) hazelnut oil or extra-virgin olive oil

Kosher salt and freshly ground pepper

3 tablespoons white balsamic vinegar

2 Granny Smith apples

Preheat the oven to 375°F (190°C).

Spread the hazelnuts in a shallow pan, place in the oven, and toast, stirring once or twice, until crisp, fragrant, and brown, about 10 minutes. Wrap the hot nuts in a kitchen towel and let steam for 1 minute, then vigorously roll the wrapped nuts between the palms of your hands until most of the dark brown skins are removed. Pick the nuts out of the debris of the peels and coarsely chop them. (The nuts can be toasted and skinned 1 day ahead of time. Store them in an airtight container at room temperature.)

In a large bowl, toss together the watercress and endive. Drizzle with the oil and toss well. Sprinkle about ½ teaspoon salt over the greens and toss again. Add the hazelnuts, vinegar, and about ½ teaspoon pepper and toss well. Taste and adjust the seasoning.

Halve and core the apples and cut each half lengthwise into eighths. Add the apple slices to the bowl with the greens and toss to mix. Serve right away.

Butternut Squash Soup

PREP TIME 25 MINUTES **COOK TIME** 1 HOUR, 5 MINUTES
SERVES 8–10

3 tablespoons canola oil

2 tablespoons balsamic vinegar

2 butternut squashes, about 3 lb (1.5 kg) total weight, halved lengthwise and seeded

1 large Granny Smith apple or Anjou or Bosc pear, peeled, halved, and cored

2 yellow onions, quartered

6 cups (48 fl oz/1.5 l) Chicken Stock (page 106) or low-sodium chicken broth

¼ teaspoon freshly grated nutmeg

½ cup (4 fl oz/125 ml) half-and-half or ½ cup (4 oz/125 g) plain yogurt

Kosher salt and freshly ground pepper

1 tablespoon unsalted butter

¼ cup (⅓ oz/10 g) chopped fresh sage

Preheat the oven to 450°F (230°C). Line a rimmed baking sheet with aluminum foil.

In a small bowl, stir together the oil and vinegar. Brush the cut sides of the squash, the apple halves, and the onions with the oil mixture. Place the squash and apple halves, cut side down, and the onions on the prepared baking sheet. Roast, turning the fruit and vegetables twice, until tender and lightly browned, about 30 minutes for the apple and 45–50 minutes for the vegetables. Transfer to a cutting board and let cool. Scoop out the flesh from the squash halves, discarding the peel. Coarsely chop the apple and onions.

Transfer the squash flesh, apple, and onions to a large saucepan and add the stock and nutmeg. Bring to a boil over medium-high heat and then reduce the heat to medium. Simmer until very tender, about 20 minutes. Remove from the heat and let cool slightly.

In a blender, purée the soup in batches until smooth. Return the soup to the pan, stir in the half-and-half, season to taste with salt and pepper, and heat through over medium heat. (The soup can be prepared up to 2 days in advance and stored, tightly covered, in the refrigerator.)

Just before serving, in a small frying pan over medium heat, melt the butter. Add the sage and sauté until the butter browns lightly and the sage is crisp. Ladle the soup into warmed bowls, garnish with the sage, and serve right away.

Shrimp Bisque

PREP TIME 20 MINUTES **COOK TIME** 40 MINUTES
SERVES 8

4 tablespoons (2 oz/60 g) unsalted butter

2 lb (1 kg) small shrimp, peeled and deveined, shells reserved

1¼ cups (6 oz/185 g) finely chopped carrot

½ cup (2½ oz/75 g) finely chopped celery

½ cup (2½ oz/75 g) finely chopped shallot

1 teaspoon finely chopped fresh thyme, plus more for garnish

2 tablespoons all-purpose flour

4 cups (32 fl oz/1 l) Chicken Stock (page 106) or low-sodium chicken broth

¾ cup (6 fl oz/180 ml) medium-dry sherry

1 can (14½ oz/455 g) crushed tomatoes

½ cup (4 fl oz/125 ml) heavy cream

2 large egg yolks

Kosher salt and freshly ground pepper

In a large saucepan over low heat, melt the butter. Add the shrimp shells, carrot, celery, shallot, and the 1 teaspoon thyme. Cover and cook, stirring once or twice, until the vegetables are softened and the mixture is fragrant, about 10 minutes.

Uncover the pan, sprinkle the flour over the shell mixture, and cook uncovered, stirring once or twice, for 2 minutes. Do not allow the mixture to brown. Gradually stir in the stock and sherry. Bring to a simmer, cover partially, and cook, stirring occasionally, for 15 minutes to blend the flavors.

Pour the soup mixture through a fine-mesh sieve set over a bowl and press hard with the back of a spoon to extract all the liquid from the solids. There should be 4 cups (32 fl oz/1 l) liquid. Discard the solids. (The soup can be prepared through this step 1 day ahead of time. Let cool, cover, and refrigerate, returning it to room temperature before proceeding with the recipe.)

Wipe the pan clean, return the strained liquid to it, and set it over medium-low heat. Stir in the shrimp and tomatoes. In a small bowl, thoroughly whisk together the cream and egg yolks. Stir the cream mixture, ¾ teaspoon salt, and ½ teaspoon pepper into the pan. Cook, stirring often, until the soup is steaming and thickened and the shrimp are pink, curled, and just cooked through, 10–12 minutes. Do not allow the mixture to boil. Taste and adjust the seasoning.

Ladle the soup into warmed shallow bowls, garnish with thyme, and serve right away.

Cream of Chestnut Soup

PREP TIME 20 MINUTES **COOK TIME** 25 MINUTES
SERVES 8–10

2 small heads escarole

½ cup (4 oz/125 g) unsalted butter

4 shallots, chopped

4 ribs celery, chopped

3 lb (1.5 kg) vacuum-packed peeled chestnuts

2 cups (16 fl oz/500 ml) heavy cream

6 cups (48 fl oz/1.5 l) Chicken Stock (page 106) or low-sodium chicken broth

Kosher salt and freshly ground white pepper

¼ cup (2 fl oz/60 ml) dry sherry

Remove 2 very pale green leaves from the escarole heads. Roll up the leaves lengthwise and cut crosswise into thin strips. Set aside. Coarsely chop the remaining escarole.

In a large saucepan over medium heat, melt the butter. Add the shallots, celery, and chopped escarole, reduce the heat to low, cover, and cook, stirring occasionally, until the vegetables are translucent, about 5 minutes (do not let them brown). Add the chestnuts and cook until soft, 8–10 minutes. Add the cream and stock and simmer until the flavors are blended, about 10 minutes.

Working in batches, transfer the contents of the pan to a blender and carefully purée until smooth. Strain the soup through a fine-mesh sieve into a clean large saucepan; discard the solids in the sieve.

Reheat the soup over low heat, being careful not to let it boil. Season to taste with salt and pepper. Stir in the sherry.

Ladle the soup into a large warmed soup tureen or warmed individual bowls. Garnish with the escarole strips and serve right away.

Carrot Soup with Orange & Ginger

PREP TIME 20 MINUTES **COOK TIME** 30 MINUTES
SERVES 8

3 tablespoons olive oil

2 leeks, white and light green parts, thinly sliced

6 carrots, about 1 lb (500 g) total weight, peeled and thinly sliced

1 red potato, about ½ lb (250 g), peeled and diced

1½ teaspoons peeled and minced fresh ginger

5 cups (40 fl oz/1.25 l) Chicken Stock (page 106), Vegetable Stock (page 106) or low-sodium chicken or vegetable broth

½ cup (4 fl oz/125 ml) fresh orange juice

2 teaspoons grated orange zest

Kosher salt and freshly ground pepper

8 thin orange slices for garnish

In a large saucepan over medium heat, warm the oil. Add the leeks and sauté until slightly softened, about 3 minutes. Add the carrots, potato, and ginger and sauté until the vegetables are just softened, about 5 minutes longer.

Add the stock, cover partially, and simmer until the vegetables are completely softened, about 20 minutes. Remove from the heat and let cool slightly.

In a blender or food processor, purée the soup in batches, leaving some texture, and return the soup to the pan. Return the soup to medium heat and stir in the orange juice and zest. Season to taste with salt and pepper.

Ladle the soup into warmed bowls, garnish each serving with an orange slice, and serve right away.

Main Dishes

Classic Roasted Turkey 29

Curry-Spiced Turkey 29

Cider-Brined, Spice-Rubbed Turkey 30

Roasted Turkey with Herb Butter 33

Spatchcocked Turkey with Herb Glaze 33

*Grill-Roasted Turkey with
Orange-Fennel Pan Gravy 34*

Baked Ham with Honey-Port Glaze 35

Vegetable Potpie 35

Classic Roasted Turkey

PREP TIME 10 MINUTES   **INACTIVE PREP TIME** 1½ HOURS
COOK TIME 2½–3½ HOURS   **SERVES** 12–14

1 turkey, 16–18 lb (8–9 kg)
Olive oil
Kosher salt and freshly ground pepper

Fresh herbs, such as thyme or rosemary sprigs or bay leaves (optional)
½ cup (4 oz/125 g) unsalted butter, melted and cooled

Remove the neck and giblets from the turkey and discard or save for another use. Pat the turkey thoroughly dry with paper towels.

Drizzle the turkey with oil, then use your hands to spread it all over the skin of the bird. Sprinkle the skin generously with salt and pepper. Tuck the wings behind the back. Place the turkey, breast side up, on a rack in a large roasting pan. Truss the legs with kitchen string (see page 100), if desired. If using herbs, strew them over and around the bird. Let the turkey stand at room temperature for 1 hour.

Position a rack in the lower third of the oven and preheat to 400°F (200°C).

Put the turkey in the oven and roast for 30 minutes. Reduce the oven temperature to 325°F (165°C). Continue to roast, brushing the turkey with the butter and the pan juices every 30 minutes, until the skin is golden brown all over, 2–3 hours more. To test for doneness, insert an instant-read thermometer into the thickest part of the breast and thigh away from the bone. The breast should register 165°F (74°C) and the thigh 175°F (80°C).

Transfer the turkey to a carving board, cover loosely with aluminum foil, and let rest for 20–30 minutes before carving.

Curry-Spiced Turkey

PREP TIME 15 MINUTES   **INACTIVE PREP TIME** 5½ HOURS
COOK TIME 2–3 HOURS   **SERVES** 12–14

1 tablespoon fennel seeds
¾ teaspoon red pepper flakes
3 tablespoons Madras curry powder
2 tablespoons sugar

1 tablespoon sweet paprika
1 tablespoon kosher salt
⅓ cup (3 fl oz/80 ml) olive oil
1 turkey, 16–18 lb (8–9 kg)

In a small, dry frying pan over medium heat, toast the fennel seeds until lightly browned and fragrant, about 1 minute. Transfer to a spice grinder, add the pepper flakes, and pulse until the mixture is finely ground. Place the mixture in a small bowl and stir in the curry powder, sugar, paprika, and salt. Stir in the oil.

Remove the neck and giblets from the turkey and discard or save for another use. Pat the turkey thoroughly dry with paper towels.

Coat the whole turkey with the spice mixture, massaging it thoroughly into the skin and inside both the neck and body cavities. Refrigerate for at least 4 hours or up to 12 hours.

Let the turkey stand at room temperature for 1 hour.

Position a rack in the lower third of the oven and preheat to 325°F (165°C).

Place the turkey, breast side up, on a rack in a large roasting pan and place in the oven. Roast the turkey, basting every 20 minutes with the pan juices, until the skin is golden brown all over, 2–3 hours. To test for doneness, insert an instant-read thermometer into the thickest part of the breast and thigh away from the bone. The breast should register 165°F (74°C) and the thigh 175°F (80°C).

Transfer the turkey to a carving board, cover loosely with aluminum foil, and let rest for 20–30 minutes before carving.

Cider-Brined, Spice-Rubbed Turkey

PREP TIME 30 MINUTES **INACTIVE PREP TIME** 37½ HOURS
COOK TIME 2½–3 HOURS **SERVES** 8–12

1 turkey, 12–14 lb (6–7 kg)

FOR THE BRINE
8 cups (64 fl oz/2 l) apple cider
¾ cup (6 oz/185 g) kosher salt
1 cup (8 fl oz/250 ml) sorghum syrup or maple syrup
2 bay leaves
2 fresh rosemary sprigs
3 fresh thyme sprigs
6 juniper berries
5 allspice berries

FOR THE SPICE RUB
¼ cup (2 oz/60 g) sumac
2 tablespoons kosher salt
2 tablespoons turmeric
2 teaspoons ground cinnamon
½ teaspoon freshly ground pepper
¼ teaspoon ground cloves

¼ cup (2 fl oz/60 ml) olive oil or canola oil

Remove the neck and giblets from the turkey and discard or save for another use.

To make the brine, in a large saucepan over high heat, combine 8 cups (64 fl oz/2 l) water, the cider, salt, and sorghum syrup. Bring to a boil, stirring to dissolve the salt. Remove from the heat. Add the bay leaves, rosemary, thyme, juniper berries, and allspice to the pan. Let the brine cool to room temperature.

Place the turkey in a large nonaluminum pot or brining bag. Carefully add the brine to the pot, plus enough water to submerge the turkey completely in liquid. Cover and refrigerate for 24–36 hours.

Remove the turkey from the brine, rinse with cold water, and pat thoroughly dry with paper towels. Place the turkey on a large rimmed baking sheet. Refrigerate, uncovered, for 12 hours.

About 1 hour before you are ready to cook, remove the turkey from the refrigerator and let stand at room temperature.

Position a rack in the lower third of the oven and preheat to 450°F (230°C).

To make the spice rub, in a bowl, combine the sumac, salt, turmeric, cinnamon, pepper, and cloves.

Brush the turkey all over with the oil and use your hands to rub the spice rub evenly over the surface of the bird. Place the turkey, breast side up, on a rack in a large roasting pan. Place the bird in the oven and reduce the oven temperature to 400°F (200°C). Roast for 30 minutes.

Reduce the oven temperature to 350°F (180°C). Continue to roast until the skin is golden brown all over, 2–2½ hours more. To test for doneness, insert an instant-read thermometer into the thickest part of the breast and thigh away from the bone. The breast should register 165°F (74°C) and the thigh 175°F (80°C).

Transfer the turkey to a carving board, cover loosely with aluminum foil, and let rest for 20–30 minutes before carving.

Note: This recipe was created by Sam Beall, proprietor of Tennessee's Blackberry Farm.

Roasted Turkey with Herb Butter

PREP TIME 15 MINUTES   **INACTIVE PREP TIME** 1½ HOURS
COOK TIME 3–3¾ HOURS   **SERVES** 12

1 turkey, about 16 lb (8 kg)	2 teaspoons kosher salt
½ cup (4 oz/125 g) unsalted butter, at room temperature	½ teaspoon freshly ground pepper
2 tablespoons mixed chopped fresh herbs, such as thyme, rosemary, and sage	1 tablespoon Marsala

Let the turkey stand at room temperature for 1 hour.

Position a rack in the lower third of the oven and preheat to 400°F (200°C).

Using an electric mixer on medium speed, beat together the butter, herbs, salt, pepper, and Marsala until well blended, 1–2 minutes. Set aside.

Remove the neck and giblets from the turkey and discard or save for another use. Pat the turkey dry with paper towels.

Gently slide your fingers between the skin and flesh on the turkey breasts on both sides of the breastbone to loosen the skin. Work your fingers down to the thigh, being careful not to tear the skin.

Spread one-third of the butter mixture evenly under the skin, using your hands to massage it evenly over the flesh. Next, spread one-third of the butter mixture inside the body cavity. Finally, spread the remaining butter mixture over the skin of the turkey, coating it evenly.

Place the turkey, breast side up, on a rack in a roasting pan and roast for 45 minutes. Reduce the oven temperature to 325°F (165°C) and continue to roast, basting every 30 minutes with pan juices. After 2½ hours of total roasting time, begin testing for doneness by inserting an instant-read thermometer into the thickest part of the breast and thigh away from the bone. The breast should register 165°F (74°C) and the thigh 175°F (80°C). If the breast begins to cook too quickly, tent it loosely with aluminum foil. The total roasting time should be 3–3¾ hours.

Transfer the turkey to a carving board, cover loosely with foil, and let rest for 20–30 minutes before carving.

Spatchcocked Turkey with Herb Glaze

PREP TIME 20 MINUTES   **INACTIVE PREP TIME** 7½ HOURS
COOK TIME 2½–2¾ HOURS   **SERVES** 8–12

1 turkey, 12–14 lb (6–7 kg)	3 tablespoons minced fresh rosemary
Kosher salt and freshly ground pepper	3 tablespoons Dijon mustard
6 cloves garlic, minced	3 tablespoons fresh lemon juice
¼ cup (1½ oz/45 g) minced shallot	3 tablespoons extra-virgin olive oil
⅓ cup (½ oz/15 g) minced fresh flat-leaf parsley	1–2 tablespoons unsalted butter, melted
3 tablespoons minced fresh oregano	

Remove the neck and giblets from the turkey and discard or save for another use. Pat the turkey thoroughly dry with paper towels.

Follow the instructions on page 100 to spatchcock the turkey. Season the bird on both sides with salt and pepper.

In a bowl, mix together the garlic, shallot, parsley, oregano, rosemary, mustard, lemon juice, and oil. Gently slide your fingers between the skin and flesh on the turkey breasts on both sides of the breastbone to loosen the skin. Work your fingers down to the thigh, being careful not to tear the skin. Use your fingers to push some of the herb mixture under the skin of the breast and thighs, massaging it evenly over the flesh. Rub the remaining herb mixture over the surface of the bird. Place the turkey on a rimmed baking sheet, cover loosely with plastic wrap, and refrigerate for 6–24 hours.

Let the turkey stand at room temperature for 1 hour.

Position a rack in the lower third of the oven and preheat to 375°F (190°C). Spray a roasting pan with nonstick cooking spray and place a rack in the pan.

Place the turkey, breast side up, on the rack and tuck the legs in tightly. Brush with the melted butter. Roast until the skin is golden brown all over and an instant-read thermometer inserted (away from the bone) into the thickest part of the breast registers 165°F (74°C) and into the thigh registers 175°F (80°C), 2½–2¾ hours.

Transfer the turkey to a carving board, cover loosely with aluminum foil, and let rest for 20–30 minutes before carving.

Grill-Roasted Turkey with Orange-Fennel Pan Gravy

PREP TIME 30 MINUTES   **INACTIVE PREP TIME** 13½ HOURS
COOK TIME 2½–3 HOURS   **SERVES** 8–12

FOR THE ORANGE BRINE
4 large oranges
6 cups (48 fl oz/1.5 l) fresh orange juice
½ cup (4 oz/125 g) kosher salt
10 whole cloves
3 tablespoons fennel seeds
2 cinnamon sticks, broken in half

1 turkey, 12–14 lb (6–7 kg)

Coarsely ground pepper
2 fennel bulbs, trimmed and coarsely sliced
1 large orange
2 tablespoons olive oil
4–6 cups (32–48 fl oz/1–1.5 l) Chicken Stock (page 106) or low-sodium chicken broth
Kosher salt and freshly ground pepper

To make the orange brine, using a vegetable peeler, remove the zest from the oranges in strips, being careful to cut away only the colored part and leaving the bitter white pith behind. Place the zest in a large saucepan. Squeeze the juice from the oranges and add it to the saucepan along with the 6 cups (48 fl oz/1.5 l) orange juice, the salt, cloves, fennel seeds, and cinnamon sticks.

Bring the liquid to a boil over medium-high heat, stirring to dissolve the salt. Remove from the heat and let cool completely.

Transfer the brine to a deep, nonaluminum 5-gallon (20-l) container. Remove the neck and giblets from the turkey and discard or reserve for another use. Add the turkey to the brine, and then add enough water to submerge the turkey completely in liquid. Cover and refrigerate for 12–24 hours.

About 1 hour before you are ready to cook, remove the turkey from the refrigerator and let stand at room temperature.

Prepare a charcoal or gas grill for indirect-heat cooking over medium heat (see page 107). Remove the turkey from the brine and pat thoroughly dry with paper towels.

Discard the brine. Season the bird inside and out with the coarse pepper, then stuff half of the fennel into the cavity. Using a vegetable peeler, remove the zest from the orange in strips, being careful to cut away only the colored part and leaving the bitter white pith behind. Put half of the zest into the cavity of the turkey. With your fingers, pull off most of the white pith from the orange, then pull the fruit into sections. Place half of the sections in the cavity. Truss the legs with kitchen string (see page 100). Brush the turkey all over with the oil.

Place the remaining fennel and orange zest and sections in a heavy-duty, aluminum foil pan large enough to hold the turkey. Place the turkey, breast side up, on the fennel and orange sections. Pour 1 cup (8 fl oz/250 ml) of the stock into the pan.

Place the pan on the grill rack away from the fire. Cover the grill and grill-roast the turkey, adding more coals as needed if you are using a charcoal grill, until the skin is a rich golden brown, 2½–3 hours. Baste with the drippings or broth every 30 minutes and add additional broth to the pan as needed to prevent the drippings from burning. If the turkey wings begin to burn during cooking, tent them with aluminum foil. To test for doneness, insert an instant-read thermometer into the thickest part of the breast and thigh away from the bone. The breast should register 165°F (74°C) and the thigh 175°F (80°C).

Transfer the turkey to a carving board, cover loosely with aluminum foil, and let rest for 20–30 minutes while you make the pan gravy.

Skim the fat from the pan drippings, leaving about 2 tablespoons in the pan. Place the aluminum foil pan back on the grill rack directly over the coals or heat elements. Add 3 cups (24 fl oz/ 750 ml) of the stock to the pan and bring to a simmer, scraping up the browned bits on the bottom of the pan. Simmer, stirring the fennel into the stock and mashing it with the back of a large spoon to thicken the liquid slightly, until the liquid reduces to a light gravy consistency, about 10 minutes. Season to taste with salt and pepper. If desired, stir some of the fennel, orange zest, and orange sections from the turkey cavity into the gravy.

Carve the turkey and serve with the gravy.

Baked Ham with Honey-Port Glaze

PREP TIME 10 MINUTES   **INACTIVE PREP TIME** 15 MINUTES
COOK TIME 2¼ HOURS   **SERVES** 6–8

1 fully cooked bone-in ham, about 8 lb (4 kg)

½ cup (3½ oz/105 g) firmly packed golden brown sugar

¼ cup (3 oz/90 g) honey

2 teaspoons dry mustard

¾ cup (6 fl oz/180 ml) port

Position a rack in the lower third of the oven and preheat to 325°F (165°C).

Using a sharp knife, score the fat on the upper half of the ham in a diamond pattern, cutting about ¼ inch (6 mm) deep. Place the ham, fat side up, on a rack in a roasting pan. Roast for 1¼ hours.

In a small bowl, mix together the brown sugar, honey, and mustard. Carefully spread half of the sugar-honey mixture over the scored surface of the ham. Stir the port into the remaining sugar-honey mixture. Continue to roast the ham, basting several times with the port mixture, until the ham is well glazed and shiny, about 1 hour longer.

Transfer the ham to a carving board and let rest for 15 minutes before carving.

Vegetable Potpie

PREP TIME 45 MINUTES   **COOK TIME** 45 MINUTES
SERVES 8–10

1 Yukon gold potato, peeled

1 sweet potato, peeled

¾-lb (375-g) piece of butternut squash, peeled and seeded

2 carrots, peeled

1 parsnip, peeled

1 yellow onion

½ lb (250 g) portobello mushrooms, brushed clean and cut into thick strips

2 tablespoons olive oil

Kosher salt and freshly ground pepper

1 cup (7 oz/220 g) drained and rinsed canned cannellini beans

2½ cups (20 fl oz/625 ml) Vegetable Stock (page 106) or low-sodium vegetable broth

2 teaspoons finely chopped fresh sage

2 teaspoons finely chopped fresh thyme

2 cloves garlic, minced

2 tablespoons cornstarch

1 recipe dough for Cheddar-Chive Biscuits (page 47), rolled out and cut into rounds

Preheat the oven to 425°F (220°C).

Cut the potato, sweet potato, squash, carrots, parsnip, and onion into ¾-inch (2-cm) pieces and place in a large bowl with the mushrooms. Drizzle with the oil, sprinkle with salt and pepper, and toss to coat evenly. Spread the vegetables in a single layer on 2 large rimmed baking sheets. Roast, stirring once or twice, until light golden, about 25 minutes. Transfer the vegetables to a shallow 2½-quart (2.5-l) baking dish. Mix in the beans.

In a saucepan over high heat, combine the stock, sage, thyme, garlic, and pepper to taste and bring to a boil. Stir in the cornstarch, reduce the heat to low, and simmer until slightly thickened, about 2 minutes. Pour over the vegetables.

Top the filling with the unbaked biscuit dough rounds. Bake the potpie until the biscuits are golden brown and the filling is bubbling, 18–20 minutes. Serve right away.

Stuffings & Breads

Focaccia Stuffing with Chestnuts, Bacon & Apples

PREP TIME 35 MINUTES   **COOK TIME** 1¾ HOURS
SERVES 10–12

1 lb (500 g) loaf focaccia

¾ lb (375 g) bacon, diced

3 tablespoons extra-virgin olive oil

1 yellow onion, diced

2 ribs celery, diced

2 Gala apples, peeled, cored, and diced

1 tablespoon *each* chopped fresh flat-leaf parsley, sage, and thyme

¾ teaspoon kosher salt

Freshly ground pepper

1 cup (4 oz/125 g) coarsely chopped vacuum-packed peeled chestnuts

3–4 cups (24–32 fl oz/ 750 ml–1 l) Turkey Stock (page 106), Chicken Stock (page 106), or low-sodium poultry broth, warmed

Preheat the oven to 250°F (120°C). Butter a 2½-quart (2.5-l) or 9-by-13-inch (23-by-33-cm) baking dish. Cut the bread into ½-inch (12-mm) cubes with crust intact. (You will have about 10 cups/1 lb/500 g of cubes.) Spread the bread cubes on 2 rimmed baking sheets and dry in the oven for 40 minutes. Remove from the oven and set aside. Raise the oven temperature to 375°F (190°C).

In a large sauté pan over medium heat, sauté the bacon until crisp and browned, about 10 minutes. Using a slotted spoon, transfer the bacon to a paper towel–lined plate to drain. Discard all but 1 tablespoon of the bacon fat in the pan.

In the same pan over medium heat, warm the oil with the bacon fat. Add the onion, celery, apples, herbs, salt, and pepper to taste, and sauté until the vegetables and apples are soft and translucent, about 10 minutes. Stir in the chestnuts and bacon. Transfer the mixture to a very large bowl, add the bread cubes, and stir until well mixed. Stir in the stock ½ cup (4 fl oz/125 ml) at a time, making sure it is completely absorbed into the bread and has not pooled in the bottom of the bowl. Taste a bread cube; it should be moist throughout but not mushy. You may not need all of the stock.

Transfer the mixture to the prepared baking dish. Cover with a lid or buttered sheet of aluminum foil and bake for 20 minutes. Uncover and continue baking until the top is golden brown and crisp, 25–35 minutes more.

Let rest for about 10 minutes before serving.

Spicy Corn Bread Stuffing with Chorizo & Pepitas

PREP TIME 45 MINUTES   **COOK TIME** 2 HOURS
SERVES 10–12

1 recipe Buttermilk Corn Bread (page 46), cooled

5 tablespoons (3 fl oz/80 ml) extra-virgin olive oil

1 lb (500 g) Mexican-style fresh chorizo (not Spanish-style cured chorizo)

1 yellow onion, diced

3 ribs celery, diced

1 large jalapeño chile, seeded and finely chopped

½ teaspoon ground cumin

¾ teaspoon kosher salt

¼ teaspoon chipotle chile powder

Freshly ground pepper

2 tablespoons chopped fresh cilantro or flat-leaf parsley

3–4 cups (24–32 fl oz/ 750 ml–1 l) Turkey Stock (page 106), Chicken Stock (page 106), or low-sodium poultry broth, warmed

¼ cup (1 oz/30 g) toasted pepitas (pumpkin seeds)

Preheat the oven to 250°F (120°C). Butter a 9-by-13-inch (23-by-33-cm) baking dish. Use your fingers to crumble the corn bread into large bite-sized pieces with crust intact. (You will have about 10 cups/1 lb/500 g.) Spread the corn bread pieces and crumbs on 2 rimmed baking sheets and dry in the oven for 45 minutes. Remove from the oven and set aside. Raise the oven temperature to 375°F (190°C).

In a frying pan over medium-high heat, warm 2 tablespoons of the oil. Add the chorizo and cook, breaking it up into small pieces with a spatula, until browned, about 6 minutes. Transfer the chorizo to a paper towel–lined plate to drain.

In the same pan over medium-high heat, warm the remaining 3 tablespoons oil. Add the onion, celery, jalapeño, cumin, salt, chile powder, and pepper to taste and sauté until the vegetables are soft, 8–10 minutes. Transfer the mixture to a large bowl and stir in the cilantro.

Add the bread pieces and stir to mix. Stir in the stock ½ cup (4 fl oz/125 ml) at a time, making sure it is completely absorbed into the bread. Fold in the chorizo.

Transfer the mixture to the prepared baking dish. Sprinkle evenly with the pepitas. Cover the dish with a buttered sheet of aluminum foil and bake for 20 minutes. Uncover and continue baking until the top is golden brown and crisp, about 25 minutes more. Let rest for about 10 minutes before serving.

Corn Bread Stuffing with Apples, Ham & Fennel

PREP TIME 40 MINUTES   **COOK TIME** 2 HOURS
SERVES 10–12

1 recipe Buttermilk Corn Bread (page 46), cooled

2 tablespoons extra-virgin olive oil

¾ lb (375 g) ham, cut into ¼-inch (6-mm) dice

1 fennel bulb, trimmed, cored, and diced

2 Granny Smith apples, peeled, cored, and diced

1 large leek, white and light green parts, sliced

2 tablespoons unsalted butter

2 tablespoons chopped fresh flat-leaf parsley

1 tablespoon finely chopped fresh sage

¾ teaspoon kosher salt

Freshly ground pepper

½ cup (1½ oz/45 g) thinly sliced green onions, white and green parts

4–4½ cups (32–36 fl oz/ 1–1.1 l) Turkey Stock (page 106), Chicken Stock (page 106), or low-sodium poultry broth, warmed

Preheat the oven to 250°F (120°C). Butter a 9-by-13-inch (23-by-33-cm) baking dish. Use your fingers to crumble the corn bread into large bite-sized pieces with crust intact. (You will have about 10 cups/1 lb/500 g.) Spread the corn bread pieces and crumbs on 2 rimmed baking sheets and dry in the oven for 45 minutes. Remove from the oven and set aside. Raise the oven temperature to 375°F (190°C).

In a large sauté pan over medium-high heat, warm the oil. Add the ham and cook, stirring occasionally, until browned, 6–8 minutes. Using a slotted spoon, transfer the ham to a large bowl. Add the fennel, apples, and leek to the same pan over medium heat and cook, without stirring, for 2 minutes. Add the butter, parsley, sage, salt, and pepper to taste and cook, stirring occasionally, until the fennel mixture is golden, 4–6 minutes more. Transfer to the bowl with the ham.

Add the bread pieces and green onions to the bowl and stir until well mixed. Stir in the stock ½ cup (4 fl oz/125 ml) at a time, making sure it is completely absorbed into the bread.

Transfer the mixture to the prepared baking dish. Cover the dish with a buttered sheet of aluminum foil and bake for 20 minutes. Uncover and continue baking until the top is golden brown and crisp, about 25 minutes more.

Let rest for about 10 minutes before serving.

Gluten-Free Stuffing with Bacon & Kale

PREP TIME 35 MINUTES   **COOK TIME** 1¾ HOURS
SERVES 10–12

1 lb (500 g) loaf country-style gluten-free bread

4 tablespoons (2 fl oz/60 ml) extra-virgin olive oil

2 bunches kale, stems removed and leaves coarsely chopped

¾ teaspoon kosher salt

1 lb (500 g) bacon, diced

1 yellow onion, diced

3 ribs celery, diced

2 tablespoons chopped fresh flat-leaf parsley

1 tablespoon chopped fresh thyme

1½ teaspoons chopped fresh rosemary

Freshly ground pepper

3–4 cups (24–32 fl oz/ 750 ml–1 l) Turkey Stock (page 106), Chicken Stock (page 106), or low-sodium poultry broth, warmed

Preheat the oven to 250°F (120°C). Butter a 9-by-13-inch (23-by-33-cm) baking dish. Cut the bread into ½-inch (12-mm) cubes with crust intact. (You should have about 10 cups of cubes.) Spread the bread cubes on 2 rimmed baking sheets and dry in the oven for 40 minutes. Remove from the oven and set aside. Raise the oven temperature to 375°F (190°C).

In a large sauté pan over medium-high heat, warm 1 tablespoon of the oil. Add the kale and ½ teaspoon of the salt, cover, and cook, stirring once or twice, until the kale is wilted but still green, 3–5 minutes. Transfer to a large bowl. In the same pan, warm 1 tablespoon of the oil. Add the bacon and cook, stirring, until browned, about 10 minutes. Transfer to a paper towel–lined plate to drain. Discard all but 1 tablespoon of fat in the pan.

In the same pan over medium-high heat, add the remaining 2 tablespoons oil. Add the onion, celery, parsley, thyme, rosemary, the remaining ¼ teaspoon salt, and pepper to taste and sauté until the vegetables are soft, 8–10 minutes. Add the onion mixture to the bowl with the kale. Add the bread cubes and stir until well combined. Stir in the stock ½ cup (4 fl oz/ 125 ml) at a time, making sure it is completely absorbed into the bread cubes. Fold in the bacon.

Transfer the mixture to the prepared baking dish. Cover the dish with a buttered sheet of aluminum foil and bake for 20 minutes. Uncover and continue baking until the top is golden brown and crisp, about 25 minutes more. Let rest for about 10 minutes before serving.

Leek & Mushroom Stuffing

PREP TIME 30 MINUTES **COOK TIME** 1¾ HOURS

SERVES 10–12

1 lb (500 g) loaf herb or plain focaccia

5 tablespoons (3 fl oz/80 ml) extra-virgin olive oil

1½ lb (750 g) assorted mushrooms, such as king trumpet or shiitake (stems discarded if using shiitake), brushed clean and sliced

1 teaspoon kosher salt

3 large leeks, white and light green parts, thinly sliced

3 ribs celery, diced

3 tablespoons minced fresh flat-leaf parsley

1 tablespoon chopped fresh thyme

Freshly ground pepper

3–4 cups (24–32 fl oz/ 750 ml–1 l) Turkey Stock (page 106), Chicken Stock (page 106), or low-sodium poultry broth, warmed

Preheat the oven to 250°F (120°C). Butter a 9-by-13-inch (23-by-33-cm) baking dish. Cut the bread into ½-inch (12-mm) cubes with crust intact. (You should have about 10 cups of cubes.) Spread the bread cubes on 2 rimmed baking sheets and dry in the oven for 40 minutes. Remove from the oven and set aside. Raise the oven temperature to 375°F (190°C).

In a large sauté pan over medium-high heat, warm 2 tablespoons of the oil. Add the mushrooms and sauté until browned, about 10 minutes. Season with ½ teaspoon of the salt. Transfer to a very large bowl.

In the same pan over medium-high heat, warm the remaining 3 tablespoons oil. Add the leeks, celery, parsley, thyme, the remaining ½ teaspoon salt, and pepper to taste. Sauté until the vegetables are soft and translucent, 8–10 minutes. Transfer to the bowl with the mushrooms.

Add the bread cubes to the bowl and stir until well mixed. Stir in the stock ½ cup (4 fl oz/125 ml) at a time, making sure it is completely absorbed into the bread and has not pooled in the bottom of the bowl. Taste a bread cube; it should be moist throughout but not mushy. You may not need all of the stock.

Transfer the mixture to the prepared baking dish. Cover the dish with a buttered sheet of aluminum foil and bake for 20 minutes. Uncover and continue baking until the top is golden brown and crisp, about 25 minutes more.

Let rest for about 10 minutes before serving.

Oyster & Mushroom Stuffing

PREP TIME 20 MINUTES **COOK TIME** 1 HOUR

SERVES 10–12

¾ cup (6 oz/185 g) unsalted butter

2 large yellow onions, about 1 lb (500 g) total weight, finely chopped

2 cups (10 oz/315 g) finely chopped celery, including some leaves

1 tablespoon poultry seasoning

1 teaspoon dried thyme

Kosher salt and freshly ground pepper

½ lb (250 g) small cremini or white mushrooms, brushed clean and sliced

24 oysters, shucked (reserve the liquor), or 1 lb (500 g) shucked oysters, drained

2 lb (1 kg) firm country bread, cut into ½-inch (12-mm) cubes with crust intact

½ cup (¾ oz/20 g) minced fresh flat-leaf parsley

½ cup (4 fl oz/125 ml) oyster liquor or low-sodium chicken broth

Preheat the oven to 375°F (190°C). Butter a 9-by-13-inch (23-by-33-cm) baking dish.

In a large frying pan over medium heat, melt ½ cup (4 oz/ 125 g) of the butter. Add the onions and celery and sauté until soft, about 10 minutes. Stir in the poultry seasoning and thyme. Season to taste with salt and pepper. Transfer to a large bowl.

In the same pan over medium heat, melt the remaining 4 tablespoons (2 oz/60 g) butter. Add the mushrooms and sauté until glazed, about 2 minutes. Transfer to the bowl with the onion-celery mixture. Cut the oysters into bite-sized pieces and add to the bowl along with the bread cubes and parsley. Drizzle with the oyster liquor and toss gently.

Transfer the mixture to the prepared baking dish. Cover the dish with a buttered sheet of aluminum foil and bake for 20 minutes. Uncover and continue baking until the top is golden brown and crisp, about 25 minutes more.

Let rest for about 10 minutes before serving.

Apple, Celery & Sourdough Stuffing

PREP TIME 25 MINUTES **COOK TIME** 1 HOUR, 40 MINUTES
SERVES 8–10

1 lb (500 g) loaf sourdough bread, cut into ½-inch (12-mm) cubes with crust intact

¾ cup (6 oz/185 g) unsalted butter

2 large yellow onions, finely chopped

1½ cups (7½ oz/235 g) finely chopped celery, including some leaves

2 large Granny Smith apples, cored and diced

2 tablespoons chopped fresh sage, or 1 teaspoon dried sage

1 teaspoon dried thyme

½ teaspoon freshly grated nutmeg

Kosher salt

½ teaspoon freshly ground pepper

⅓ cup (½ oz/15 g) minced fresh flat-leaf parsley

3 large eggs, lightly beaten

2½ cups (20 fl oz/625 ml) Turkey Stock (page 106), Chicken Stock (page 106), or low-sodium poultry broth

Preheat the oven to 250°F (120°C). Lightly butter a 4-quart (4-l) baking dish.

Spread the bread cubes on 2 rimmed baking sheets and dry in the oven for 40 minutes. Remove from the oven and set aside. Raise the oven temperature to 375°F (190°C).

In a large frying pan over medium heat, melt 3 tablespoons of the butter. Add the onions and celery and sauté until soft, about 10 minutes. Transfer to a large bowl. In the same pan over medium heat, melt 2 tablespoons of the butter. Add the apples and sauté until glazed, about 5 minutes. Transfer to the bowl with the onion-celery mixture. Add the sage, thyme, nutmeg, salt to taste, and the pepper and mix well. In the same pan over medium heat, melt the remaining 7 tablespoons (3½ oz/105 g) butter. Add the bread cubes and parsley and toss to coat. Transfer to the bowl. In another bowl, combine the eggs and stock and whisk until blended. Pour the stock mixture over the bread mixture and toss gently.

Transfer the mixture to the prepared baking dish. Cover the dish with a buttered sheet of aluminum foil and bake for 20 minutes. Uncover and continue baking until the top is golden brown and crisp, about 25 minutes more.

Let rest for about 10 minutes before serving.

Quinoa & Red Rice Stuffing with Kale & Pine Nuts

PREP TIME 20 MINUTES **COOK TIME** 1 HOUR
SERVES 8–10

1½ cups (11 oz/345 g) red rice

1½ cups (11 oz/345 g) quinoa

4 tablespoons (2 oz/60 g) unsalted butter

1 large yellow onion, diced

2 ribs celery, diced

1 bunch Tuscan kale, stems removed and leaves thinly sliced

2 cloves garlic, minced

1 tablespoon chopped fresh oregano

Kosher salt and freshly ground pepper

½ cup (2 oz/60 g) dried cranberries, coarsely chopped

½ cup (2½ oz/75 g) pine nuts, toasted

Zest of 1 lemon

1 cup (8 fl oz/250 ml) Turkey Stock (page 106), Chicken Stock (page 106), or low-sodium poultry broth, warmed

Shaved Parmesan cheese (optional)

Preheat the oven to 375°F (190°C). Lightly butter a 9-by-13-inch (23-by-33-cm) baking dish.

In a saucepan, combine the red rice with 2¼ cups (18 fl oz/560 ml) water. Set over high heat and bring to a boil. Reduce the heat to low, cover, and simmer until most of the water is absorbed and the grains are tender, about 20 minutes. Set aside. In another saucepan, combine the quinoa with 3 cups (24 fl oz/750 ml) water. Set over high heat and bring to a boil. Reduce the heat to low, cover, and simmer until most of the water is absorbed and the grains are translucent, about 15 minutes. Let stand covered for 5 minutes. Set aside.

In a large sauté pan over medium heat, melt the butter. Add the onion and celery and cook, stirring occasionally, until softened, 6–8 minutes. Add the kale and garlic during the last 2 minutes of cooking. Add the oregano and season to taste with salt and pepper. Cook, stirring, until the mixture is fragrant, about 1 minute. Transfer the onion mixture to a large bowl. Fluff the rice and quinoa with a fork, then add to the bowl along with the cranberries, pine nuts, lemon zest, and stock and stir until well combined. Season to taste with salt and pepper.

Transfer the mixture to the prepared baking dish and bake, uncovered, for 30 minutes. Let rest for 10 minutes, then garnish with cheese, if using, and serve.

Everything Parker House Rolls

PREP TIME 40 MINUTES   **INACTIVE PREP TIME** 1¾ HOURS
COOK TIME 20 MINUTES   **MAKES** 24 ROLLS

1½ cups (12 fl oz/375 ml) whole milk

½ cup (4 oz/125 g) unsalted butter, cut into 8 pieces, plus 2 tablespoons butter, melted

4½ teaspoons (½ oz/15 g) active dry yeast

4 cups (1¼ lb/625 g) all-purpose flour

3 tablespoons sugar

1 tablespoon kosher salt

Oil

1½ teaspoons Maldon or other flake sea salt

½ teaspoon dried onion flakes

½ teaspoon dried garlic flakes

1 teaspoon white sesame seeds

In a small saucepan over medium heat, combine the milk and the ½ cup (4 oz/125 g) butter. Warm until the butter has melted, about 7 minutes. Remove from the heat and let cool until the mixture registers 105°–115°F (40°–46°C) on an instant-read thermometer. Add the yeast and stir until dissolved. Let stand for 10 minutes.

In the bowl of a stand mixer fitted with the dough hook, combine the flour, sugar, and kosher salt and beat on low speed until combined, about 30 seconds. Add the milk mixture and continue to beat on low speed until the dough forms a ball, about 1 minute. Increase the speed to medium-low and knead until the dough is smooth and elastic, 4–5 minutes. Remove the dough from the mixer bowl, oil the inside of the bowl, and return the dough to the bowl. Cover the bowl tightly with plastic wrap and let the dough rise in a warm place until doubled in volume, about 1 hour. Divide the dough in half.

Grease a 9-by-13-inch (23-by-33-cm) baking pan. On a lightly floured work surface, roll each piece of dough into a log 12 inches (30 cm) long. Using a pastry scraper, divide each log into 12 equal pieces. Using the cupped palm of your hand, roll and shape each piece into a taut ball.

Arrange the dough balls in the prepared baking pan, making 4 rows of 6 balls each. Cover the pan tightly with plastic wrap and let the balls rise in a warm place for 30 minutes.

In a small bowl, combine the sea salt, onion flakes, garlic flakes, and sesame seeds.

Preheat the oven to 375°F (190°C).

Remove the plastic wrap from the pan. Brush the tops of the rolls with the melted butter and sprinkle with the sea salt mixture. Bake until the rolls are golden and an instant-read thermometer inserted into the center of a roll registers 190°F (88°C), 18–20 minutes.

Invert the rolls onto a wire rack, remove the pan, then turn the rolls right side up onto another rack. Let the rolls cool slightly before serving.

Soufflé Spoon Bread with Cheddar Cheese

PREP TIME 15 MINUTES **COOK TIME** 50 MINUTES
SERVES 8–10

2½ cups (20 fl oz/625 ml) whole milk

½ teaspoon kosher salt

½ cup (2½ oz/75 g) white cornmeal

4 tablespoons (2 oz/60 g) unsalted butter

¼ teaspoon freshly grated nutmeg

6 large eggs, separated

1 cup (4 oz/125 g) shredded extra-sharp white Cheddar cheese

Preheat the oven to 350°F (180°C). Lightly butter a 1½-quart (1.5-l) soufflé dish or baking dish.

In a saucepan over medium-high heat, combine the milk and salt and heat just until small bubbles appear along the sides of the pan. Reduce the heat to a simmer, stir in the cornmeal and cook, stirring, until the mixture thickens, about 10 minutes. Stir in the butter and nutmeg. Remove from the heat and whisk in the egg yolks and cheese. Set aside to cool slightly.

Using an electric mixer, beat the egg whites until soft peaks form. Gently fold the beaten whites into the cornmeal mixture just until no white streaks are visible. Transfer to the prepared dish. (The spoon bread can be assembled up to this point 8 hours in advance of baking. Cover and refrigerate, then bring to room temperature before continuing.)

Bake until the spoon bread is puffed and golden brown, 35–40 minutes. Serve hot.

Buttermilk Corn Bread

PREP TIME 15 MINUTES **COOK TIME** 20 MINUTES
SERVES 8–10

2 cups (14 oz/440 g) coarse-ground yellow cornmeal

1 cup (5 oz/155 g) all-purpose flour

⅓ cup (3 oz/90 g) sugar

4 teaspoons baking powder

1 teaspoon kosher salt

1½ cups (12 fl oz/375 ml) buttermilk, at room temperature

2 large eggs, at room temperature, well beaten

½ cup (4 oz/125 g) unsalted butter, melted

Preheat the oven to 400°F (200°C). Grease a 9-by-13-inch (23-by-33-cm) baking pan.

In a large bowl, stir together the cornmeal, flour, sugar, baking powder, and salt, mixing well. In another bowl, stir together the buttermilk, eggs, and butter just until mixed. Stir the wet ingredients into the dry ingredients just until combined. Spread the batter in the prepared pan.

Bake until the edges of the corn bread are just beginning to pull away from the sides of the pan and a knife inserted into the center comes out clean, 18–20 minutes. Let stand in the pan for at least 5 minutes, then carefully invert the pan onto a baking sheet.

Cut the corn bread into squares and serve warm.

Cheddar-Chive Biscuits

PREP TIME 20 MINUTES **COOK TIME** 15 MINUTES
MAKES ABOUT 18 BISCUITS

2 cups (10 oz/315 g)
all-purpose flour

2½ teaspoons baking
powder

½ teaspoon kosher salt

¾ cup (3 oz/90 g) shredded
white Cheddar cheese

⅓ cup (½ oz/15 g) minced
fresh chives

6 tablespoons (3 oz/90 g)
cold unsalted butter, cut
into chunks

¾ cup (6 fl oz/180 ml)
whole milk

Preheat the oven to 425°F (220°C). Lightly butter a rimmed baking sheet.

To make the dough by hand, in a large bowl, stir together the flour, baking powder, salt, cheese, and chives. Scatter the butter over the flour mixture and, using a pastry blender or 2 knives, cut the butter into the flour mixture until it resembles coarse crumbs. Pour in the milk and mix with a fork or rubber spatula just until the dry ingredients are evenly moistened. Transfer the dough to a lightly floured work surface and knead gently a few times until the dough clings together.

To make the dough in a stand mixer, combine the flour, baking powder, salt, cheese, and chives in the mixer bowl. Fit the mixer with the paddle attachment and mix on low speed for a few seconds until blended. Add the butter and mix on medium-low speed just until the mixture forms coarse crumbs. Add the milk and mix for a few seconds until evenly moistened. Transfer the dough to a lightly floured work surface and knead gently a few times until the dough clings together.

Roll or pat out the dough about ½ inch (12 mm) thick. Using a 2-inch (5-cm) round biscuit cutter or inverted glass dipped in flour, cut out rounds by pressing straight down and lifting straight up. Do not twist the cutter or glass or the biscuits will be lopsided. Alternatively, roll or pat out the dough into a rectangle and cut into 2-inch (5-cm) squares. Place the biscuits 1 inch (2.5 cm) apart on the prepared baking sheet.

Bake until golden brown on the edges, 15–18 minutes. Transfer to a wire rack and let cool for 10 minutes. Serve warm.

Sweet Potato Biscuits with Honey Butter

PREP TIME 30 MINUTES **COOK TIME** 1½ HOURS
MAKES 12 BISCUITS

1 orange-fleshed sweet
potato, about ½ lb (250 g)

1¼ cups (10 fl oz/310 ml)
buttermilk

2½ cups (12½ oz/390 g)
all-purpose flour

1 cup (4 oz/125 g) cake flour

5 teaspoons baking powder

4 teaspoons sugar

¾ teaspoon kosher salt

½ cup (4 oz/125 g) cold
unsalted butter, cut into
small pieces

FOR THE HONEY BUTTER
¾ cup (6 oz/185 g) unsalted
butter, at room temperature

⅓ cup (4 oz/125 g) honey

Preheat the oven to 400°F (200°C).

Prick the skin of the sweet potato several times with a fork. Place it directly on the oven rack and bake until very tender, about 1¼ hours. Let cool completely.

Position a rack in the upper third of the oven and raise the oven temperature to 450°F (230°C).

Peel the sweet potato and force it through the medium disk of a food mill or a large-mesh sieve into a bowl. Add the buttermilk and whisk until smooth.

In a large bowl, sift together the all-purpose flour, cake flour, baking powder, sugar, and salt. Scatter the butter over the flour mixture and, using a pastry blender or 2 knives, cut the butter into the flour mixture until it resembles coarse crumbs. Add the buttermilk mixture and mix until a soft, crumbly dough forms. Transfer the dough to a well-floured work surface and knead 8–10 times until it just holds together.

Roll or pat out the dough into a 6-by-12-inch (15-by-30-cm) rectangle. Using a knife, cut the dough into 12 rectangular biscuits. Transfer the biscuits to an ungreased insulated baking sheet or 2 stacked regular baking sheets.

Bake until the edges and bottoms of the biscuits are lightly browned, 12–14 minutes.

Meanwhile, make the honey butter: In a small bowl, cream together the butter and honey until light and fluffy. Serve the biscuits hot, accompanied with the honey butter.

Sides

Mashed Potatoes with Herb-Infused Cream

PREP TIME 15 MINUTES   **COOK TIME** 25 MINUTES
SERVES 8–10

4½ lb (2.25 kg) russet potatoes, peeled and cut into 2-inch (5-cm) pieces

1½ cups (12 fl oz/375 ml) heavy cream

1 teaspoon minced garlic

1 shallot, thinly sliced

1 large fresh thyme sprig

1 large fresh rosemary sprig

1 bay leaf

1 teaspoon peppercorns

½ cup (4 oz/125 g) unsalted butter, at room temperature, diced

¼ cup (⅓ oz/10 g) chopped fresh chives

Kosher salt and freshly ground pepper

Put the potatoes in a large pot, add water to cover by 3 inches (7.5 cm), and generously salt the water. Bring to a boil over medium-high heat, reduce the heat to medium-low, and simmer until the potatoes are tender when pierced, about 15 minutes.

Meanwhile, in a small saucepan over medium-high heat, combine the cream, garlic, shallot, thyme sprig, rosemary sprig, bay leaf, and peppercorns. Bring to a simmer, reduce the heat to medium, and simmer until the cream is reduced to about 1 cup (8 fl oz/250 ml), 10–12 minutes. Strain the cream through a fine-mesh sieve and keep warm.

When the potatoes are ready, drain them well. Pass the potatoes through a ricer into a large bowl. Stir in the butter, then gradually pour in the cream, stirring constantly until the potatoes are smooth and creamy. Stir in the chives. Taste and adjust the seasoning with salt and pepper. (You can cook the potatoes up to 2 days in advance and refrigerate, covered. Just before serving, pour a thin layer of milk onto the bottom of a wide pot, add the potatoes, and heat, stirring occasionally, until hot.) Serve right away.

Candied Sweet Potatoes

PREP TIME 15 MINUTES   **COOK TIME** 2 HOURS
SERVES 8–10

5 lb (2.5 kg) orange-fleshed sweet potatoes, such as Garnet

½ cup (3½ oz/105 g) firmly packed golden brown sugar

4 tablespoons (2 oz/60 g) unsalted butter, cut into small pieces

Kosher salt and freshly ground pepper

½ cup (4 fl oz/125 ml) fresh orange juice

Preheat the oven to 400°F (200°C).

Prick the skin of the sweet potatoes several times with a fork. Arrange on a baking sheet and bake until tender, about 1¼ hours. Transfer the sweet potatoes to a wire rack and let them cool to room temperature. Cover loosely and let stand overnight at room temperature to firm their texture.

Preheat the oven to 350°F (180°C). Grease a 9-by-13-inch (23-by-33-cm) baking dish.

Peel the sweet potatoes and cut them into slices ½ inch (12 mm) thick. Overlap the slices in the prepared dish. Evenly sprinkle the brown sugar and butter pieces over the sweet potatoes. Season lightly with salt. Tightly cover the dish with aluminum foil and bake until hot and steaming, about 25 minutes.

Uncover the dish. Drizzle the orange juice over the sweet potatoes. Return the dish to the oven and continue to bake, basting occasionally with the syrup that accumulates in the dish, until the top is golden, 15–20 minutes. Season generously with pepper. Serve hot.

Twice-Baked Sweet Potatoes

PREP TIME 15 MINUTES   **COOK TIME** 1¼ HOURS
SERVES 8

2 bacon slices, diced

4 medium orange-fleshed sweet potatoes

2 tablespoons firmly packed dark brown sugar

2 tablespoons all-purpose flour

2 tablespoons unsalted butter, diced, plus ½ cup (4 oz/125 g) unsalted butter, melted

½ cup (2 oz/60 g) chopped pecans

¼ cup (2 fl oz/60 ml) heavy cream

1 teaspoon ground cinnamon

¼ teaspoon freshly grated nutmeg

¾ teaspoon salt

1½ cups (3 oz/90 g) miniature marshmallows

Preheat the oven to 375°F (190°C). In a sauté pan over medium heat, sauté the bacon until crisp and browned, about 6 minutes. Transfer the bacon to a paper towel–lined plate to drain.

Using a fork, prick the skin of the sweet potatoes several times. Arrange on a rimmed baking sheet and bake until tender, about 1¼ hours. Let cool. Meanwhile, in a bowl, stir together the brown sugar and flour. Add the 2 tablespoons diced butter and, using a pastry blender or 2 knives, cut the butter into the dry ingredients until the mixture resembles coarse crumbs. Stir in the pecans and bacon to make a streusel mixture. Refrigerate until ready to use.

When the sweet potatoes are cool enough to handle, halve them lengthwise and scoop out the flesh, reserving the sweet potato skins and keeping them as intact as possible. Arrange the sweet potato skins on an aluminum foil–lined rimmed baking sheet.

In a food processor, combine the sweet potato flesh, the ½ cup melted butter, the cream, cinnamon, nutmeg, and salt and process until smooth. Spoon the sweet potato mixture back into the skins on the baking sheet. Sprinkle the streusel mixture on top, dividing evenly. Bake until the streusel is toasted, 10–15 minutes.

Remove the sweet potatoes from the oven and heat the broiler. Sprinkle the marshmallows evenly over the streusel. Broil the sweet potatoes until the marshmallows are lightly browned, about 2 minutes. Serve right away.

Herbed Potato Gratin

PREP TIME 20 MINUTES   **COOK TIME** 1¼ HOURS
SERVES 6–8

1½ cups (12 fl oz/375 ml) heavy cream

1 clove garlic, minced

1 teaspoon chopped fresh rosemary

1 teaspoon chopped fresh thyme

½ teaspoon chopped fresh sage

Kosher salt and freshly ground pepper

2 lb (1 kg) russet potatoes, peeled and sliced ½ inch (12 mm) thick

½ yellow onion, thinly sliced

3 cups (12 oz/375 g) shredded Gruyère cheese

¼ cup (1 oz/30 g) grated Parmesan cheese

Preheat the oven to 375°F (190°C). Butter an 11-inch (28-cm) gratin dish.

In a large saucepan over medium heat, combine the cream, garlic, rosemary, thyme, sage, and a pinch *each* of salt and pepper. Bring just to a boil and remove from the heat. Gently stir the potatoes into the cream mixture.

Arrange one-third of the potato slices, slightly overlapping them, in the prepared gratin dish. Sprinkle generously with salt and pepper, then top with half of the onion and one-third of the Gruyère. Repeat, using another one-third of the potato slices, salt and pepper to taste, all of the remaining onion, and another one-third of the Gruyère. Top with the remaining potatoes. Gently press down on the potatoes with a spatula. Pour the remaining cream mixture over the potatoes and sprinkle with the remaining Gruyère and all of the Parmesan.

Cover the dish with aluminum foil and bake until the potatoes are tender, about 45 minutes. Remove the foil and bake until the top is golden brown, about 20 minutes more.

Let the gratin stand for 10 minutes before serving.

Green Bean Bundles with Bacon & Brown Sugar

PREP TIME 15 MINUTES   **COOK TIME** 30 MINUTES
SERVES 8–10

1½ lb (750 g) green beans, trimmed

8 thick bacon slices

6 tablespoons (3 oz/90 g) unsalted butter, melted

Kosher salt and freshly ground pepper

¾ teaspoon garlic powder

¼ cup (2 oz/60 g) firmly packed golden brown sugar

Preheat the oven to 350°F (180°C). Line a rimmed baking sheet with parchment paper. Fill a large bowl with ice water.

Bring a saucepan of salted water to a boil over high heat. Add the green beans and cook until tender-crisp, about 4 minutes. Drain and plunge into the ice water to cool. Drain again, pat dry with paper towels, and set aside.

In a large nonstick frying pan over medium heat, cook the bacon in batches until the slices are just beginning to brown along the edges but are still very underdone and pliable, 4–6 minutes. Transfer the bacon to a paper towel–lined plate and let cool. Cut each bacon slice in half crosswise.

In a small bowl, whisk together the melted butter, 1½ teaspoons salt, and the garlic powder.

Divide the green beans into 16 equal portions, about 6 beans each. Gather each portion into a neat bundle and wrap a half-slice of bacon around the center to hold the beans together. Place the bundles on the prepared baking sheet, tucking the loose ends of the bacon underneath the bundles. Sprinkle the brown sugar evenly over the bundles and then drizzle with the butter mixture.

Roast until the bacon is cooked through and browned, 20–25 minutes. Let stand for 3–5 minutes.

Transfer the green bean bundles to a warmed platter, sprinkle lightly with pepper, and serve right away.

Tangy Braised Greens

PREP TIME 15 MINUTES   **COOK TIME** 25 MINUTES
SERVES 8–10

4 tablespoons (2 fl oz/60 ml) extra-virgin olive oil

1 yellow onion, chopped

About 4 lb (2 kg) mixed collard and mustard greens, tough stems removed

Kosher salt and freshly ground pepper

¼ cup (2 fl oz/60 ml) balsamic vinegar

In a large pot over medium heat, warm 1 tablespoon of the oil. Add the onion and sauté until soft, about 5 minutes.

Add the greens and 2 cups (16 fl oz/500 ml) water to the pot. Cover and simmer until the greens are tender, about 20 minutes. Drain thoroughly.

Return the greens to the pot over medium heat. Season to taste with salt and pepper. Drizzle with the vinegar and the remaining 3 tablespoons oil and heat through, tossing to mingle the flavors.

Transfer the greens to a platter or serving bowl and serve warm.

Green Beans with Pecans

PREP TIME 10 MINUTES **COOK TIME** 15 MINUTES
SERVES 8–10

2 lb (1 kg) green beans, trimmed and halved crosswise on the diagonal

5 tablespoons (2½ oz/75 g) unsalted butter

1 cup (4 oz/125 g) chopped pecans

¾ teaspoon kosher salt

½ teaspoon freshly ground pepper

Fill a large bowl with ice water. Bring a large saucepan of salted water to a boil over high heat. Add the green beans and cook until tender-crisp, about 4 minutes. Drain and plunge into the ice water to cool. Drain again and pat dry.

In a large frying pan over medium heat, melt the butter. Add the pecans and cook, stirring often, until the nuts are lightly browned and fragrant, about 5 minutes. Add the green beans and toss to coat with the butter. Add the salt and pepper, cover partially, and cook, tossing and stirring occasionally, until the beans are heated through, 5–6 minutes more.

Taste and adjust the seasoning with salt and pepper. Serve hot.

From-Scratch Green Bean Casserole

PREP TIME 15 MINUTES **COOK TIME** 40 MINUTES
SERVES 6–8

1¼ lb (625 g) green beans, trimmed

2 tablespoons unsalted butter

10 oz (315 g) white or cremini mushrooms, brushed clean and sliced

1 large shallot, minced

3 tablespoons all-purpose flour

1 cup (8 fl oz/250 ml) whole milk

1 cup (8 fl oz/250 ml) Chicken Stock (page 106) or low-sodium chicken broth

1 teaspoon soy sauce

Kosher salt and freshly ground pepper

¾ cup (1½ oz/45 g) prepared fried onions or shallots

Preheat the oven to 350°F (180°C). Lightly butter a 9-by-13-inch (23-by-33-cm) baking dish. Fill a large bowl with ice water.

Bring a saucepan of salted water to a boil over high heat. Add the green beans and cook until tender-crisp, about 4 minutes. Drain and plunge into the ice water to cool. Drain again, pat dry with paper towels, and set aside.

In a saucepan over medium heat, melt the butter. Add the mushrooms and sauté until they have released their juices and are starting to brown, 6–7 minutes. Stir in the shallot and sauté until softened, 2–3 minutes. Stir in the flour for 2 minutes. Slowly stir in the milk, stock, and soy sauce and then bring to a boil, stirring often. Reduce the heat to low and simmer, stirring, until the mixture is thickened, 4–5 minutes. Stir in the green beans, season with salt and pepper, and transfer the mixture to the prepared baking dish. (The casserole can be prepared to this point up to 1 day ahead, covered, and refrigerated.)

Bake until the top is golden brown and the liquid is bubbling, about 20 minutes (add 10–15 minutes if the casserole has been refrigerated). Scatter the fried onions on top and bake for about 5 minutes more to warm the onions.

Let the casserole stand for about 5 minutes before serving.

Gingered Winter Squash & Pear Purée

PREP TIME 20 MINUTES   **COOK TIME** 1¼ HOURS
SERVES 8

2 small butternut squashes, about 3 lb (1.5 kg) total weight

4 firm but ripe Anjou or Bosc pears

3 tablespoons extra-virgin olive oil

Kosher salt and freshly ground pepper

4 tablespoons (2 oz/60 g) unsalted butter

1-inch (2.5-cm) piece of fresh ginger, peeled and minced

8 fresh sage leaves, cut into thin ribbons

Preheat the oven to 400°F (200°C). Lightly oil 2 or more large rimmed baking sheets.

Cut each squash in half lengthwise, then scoop out the seeds and discard. Peel the pears, halve them, then remove the cores with a paring knife or melon baller. Brush the cut sides of the squash and pears with the oil and sprinkle lightly with salt and pepper. Place the squash halves, cut side down, on one of the prepared baking sheets. Place the pear halves, cut side down, on the other sheet. Cover the baking sheets with aluminum foil and roast until the squashes and pears are very tender when pierced with the tip of a paring knife, 30–35 minutes for the pears and 1 hour for the squashes.

Place the pears in the bowl of a stand mixer fitted with the paddle attachment. When the squash is cool enough to handle, scoop out the flesh and add it to the bowl with the pears. Discard the squash skins. Mix on medium speed until smooth. (It's okay if a few coarse pieces of pear remain, but the squash should be completely smooth.)

In a large saucepan over medium heat, melt the butter, stirring occasionally, until it just begins to brown and smell nutty, 4–5 minutes. Stir in the ginger and sage and cook, stirring, for 1 minute. Measure out 2 tablespoons of the butter mixture and set aside. Add the squash mixture to the pan and cook, stirring occasionally, just until heated through, 5–7 minutes. Taste and adjust the seasoning.

Transfer the squash mixture to a warmed serving bowl, drizzle the reserved browned butter mixture over the top, and serve right away.

Brussels Sprouts & Butternut Squash with Bacon

PREP TIME 25 MINUTES   **COOK TIME** 30 MINUTES
SERVES 6–8

¼ lb (125 g) thick-cut bacon slices, cut crosswise into ¼-inch (6-mm) pieces

1 shallot, finely chopped

2 tablespoons cider vinegar

1 tablespoon firmly packed golden brown sugar

1 teaspoon Dijon mustard

1 teaspoon chopped fresh thyme

6 tablespoons (3 fl oz/90 ml) olive oil

Kosher salt and freshly ground pepper

1½ lb (750 g) brussels sprouts, trimmed

1 small butternut squash, about 1½ lb (750 g), halved lengthwise, seeded, peeled, and cut into chunks

1 teaspoon chopped fresh sage

1 cup (4 oz/125 g) coarsely chopped vacuum-packed peeled chestnuts

In a sauté pan over medium heat, cook the bacon until browned and crisp, 8–10 minutes. Transfer to a paper towel–lined plate. Pour all but 1 tablespoon of the fat into a bowl and set aside. Add the shallot to the pan and sauté until tender, 2–3 minutes. In a small bowl, whisk together the shallot, vinegar, brown sugar, mustard, and thyme. Slowly whisk in all but 1 tablespoon of the oil and season the vinaigrette with salt and pepper.

Meanwhile, fill a large bowl with ice water. Bring a large pot of salted water to a boil over high heat. Add the brussels sprouts and cook until just tender, 4–6 minutes. Using a slotted spoon, transfer the brussels sprouts to the ice water to cool. Scoop out the sprouts, drain well, and cut in half lengthwise. Return the water to a boil, add the squash, and cook until just tender, 4–6 minutes. Transfer to the ice water, then drain.

In a large sauté pan over medium heat, warm the remaining 1 tablespoon oil. Add the squash and sauté until light golden and warmed through, 3–4 minutes. Transfer to a large bowl. In the same pan over medium-high heat, warm 2 tablespoons of the reserved bacon fat. Cook the brussels sprouts, cut side down, without moving them, for 3–4 minutes. Stir, add the sage and chestnuts, and cook for 2 minutes more. Transfer to the bowl with the squash. Add enough vinaigrette to coat the vegetables lightly, then stir in half of the bacon. Transfer to a platter, sprinkle with the remaining bacon, and serve right away.

Broccoli with Crisp Bread Crumbs

PREP TIME 15 MINUTES   **COOK TIME** 20 MINUTES
SERVES 8–10

3 large bunches broccoli (about 10 stalks)

½ cup (4 oz/125 g) plus 6 tablespoons (3 oz/90 g) unsalted butter

2 tablespoons finely grated orange zest

3 cloves garlic, finely chopped

3 cups (6 oz/185 g) fresh white bread crumbs

½ teaspoon kosher salt

Freshly ground pepper

Cut off the broccoli stems and reserve for another use. Separate the heads into florets.

Fill a large bowl with ice water. Bring a large pot of salted water to a boil over high heat and add the broccoli. Cook, stirring once or twice, until just tender, 4–6 minutes. Drain and plunge into the ice water. When cool, drain again and pat dry.

In a large frying pan over medium-high heat, melt the ½ cup (4 oz/125 g) butter. Add the orange zest and garlic and cook, stirring once or twice, until the butter begins to brown, about 3 minutes. Add the bread crumbs and stir to moisten. Cook, stirring occasionally, until crisp and golden brown, about 5 minutes. Stir in ¼ teaspoon of the salt and a generous grinding of pepper. Remove from the heat and keep warm.

Meanwhile, in a large frying pan over medium heat, melt the remaining 6 tablespoons (3 oz/90 g) butter. Add the broccoli, cover the pan, and cook, tossing and stirring occasionally, until heated through and glazed with butter, about 5 minutes. Season with the remaining ¼ teaspoon salt and a generous grinding of pepper and toss again.

Spoon the broccoli into a warmed wide serving bowl. Spoon the bread crumbs evenly over the broccoli and serve right away.

Sautéed Mushrooms with Shallots & Sherry

PREP TIME 10 MINUTES   **COOK TIME** 10 MINUTES
SERVES 4

1 lb (500 g) assorted mushrooms, brushed clean

4 tablespoons (2 fl oz/60 ml) olive oil

½ cup (2 oz/60 g) thinly sliced shallots

Kosher salt and freshly ground pepper

½ cup (4 fl oz/125 ml) dry sherry

1 teaspoon chopped fresh thyme

2 tablespoons unsalted butter

Remove the stems from the mushrooms. Thickly slice smaller mushrooms and coarsely chop larger ones. Set aside.

In a large sauté pan over medium heat, warm 2 tablespoons of the oil. Add the shallots and sauté until golden, 3–5 minutes. Transfer the shallots to a bowl.

In the same pan over medium-high heat, warm the remaining 2 tablespoons oil. Add the mushrooms and ⅛ teaspoon salt and sauté until the mushrooms begin to caramelize, 4–5 minutes. Add the sherry and deglaze the pan, stirring with a wooden spoon to scrape up the browned bits on the pan bottom. Return the shallots to the pan and add the thyme. Cook over medium-high heat, stirring, until the sherry is almost evaporated, 1–2 minutes. Add the butter and cook, stirring, until the butter glazes the mushrooms, about 1 minute more. Season to taste with salt and pepper and serve.

Brussels Sprouts with Caramelized Shallots

PREP TIME 15 MINUTES   **COOK TIME** 25 MINUTES
SERVES 6–8

2 lb (1 kg) brussels sprouts, trimmed

3 tablespoons dried currants

¼ cup (2 fl oz/60 ml) balsamic vinegar, warmed

3 tablespoons olive oil

½ lb (250 g) shallots, thinly sliced into rings

Kosher salt and freshly ground pepper

If desired, prepare a garnish: Fill a bowl with ice water. Bring a saucepan filled with water to a boil over high heat. Separate 10 brussels sprouts into individual leaves. Add the leaves to the boiling water and cook until bright green, 1–2 minutes. Drain and plunge into the ice water to cool. Drain again, pat dry with paper towels, and set aside.

Using a mandoline or the shredding blade of a food processor, thinly shave the remaining brussels sprouts. In a small bowl, combine the currants and vinegar. Set aside.

In a large sauté pan over medium heat, warm 2 tablespoons of the oil. Add the shallot rings and sauté until softened and browned, about 15 minutes. Add the currants and vinegar and cook, stirring, until the liquid has evaporated, about 2 minutes. Transfer to a bowl.

In the same pan over medium heat, warm the remaining 1 tablespoon oil. Add the shaved brussels sprouts and sauté until softened and beginning to brown, about 5 minutes. Add the shallot-currant mixture to the pan and stir until heated through, 1–2 minutes. Season to taste with salt and pepper.

Transfer the contents of the pan to a warmed serving dish. Garnish with the whole brussels sprout leaves, if using, and serve right away.

Honey-Roasted Spiced Carrots

PREP TIME 15 MINUTES   **COOK TIME** 30 MINUTES
SERVES 6–8

1 teaspoon kosher salt

½ teaspoon ground coriander

¼ teaspoon ground cumin

⅛ teaspoon cayenne pepper

3 tablespoons olive oil

3 tablespoons honey

2 tablespoons fresh lemon juice

2 bunches baby rainbow carrots, trimmed, larger carrots halved lengthwise

2 teaspoons chopped fresh flat-leaf parsley

1 teaspoon chopped fresh mint

Maldon or other flake sea salt

Preheat the oven to 425°F (220°C).

In a small bowl, stir together the kosher salt, coriander, cumin, and cayenne pepper. In another bowl, whisk together 1 tablespoon of the oil, the honey, and lemon juice.

Place the carrots on a rimmed baking sheet and drizzle with the remaining 2 tablespoons oil. Sprinkle with the spice mixture and toss to coat. Spread the carrots in a single layer and drizzle with two-thirds of the honey mixture.

Roast until the carrots are tender and beginning to brown, 30–40 minutes. Transfer to a serving dish and drizzle with the remaining honey mixture. Sprinkle with the parsley, mint, and sea salt and serve right away.

Wild Rice Pilaf with Butternut Squash

PREP TIME 20 MINUTES **COOK TIME** 1 HOUR
SERVES 6–8

2 tablespoons unsalted butter

1 small sweet onion, chopped

2 teaspoons curry powder

2 cups (12 oz/375 g) wild rice

1 cinnamon stick

1 orange zest strip, about 3 inches (7.5 cm) long and ½ inch (12 mm) wide

4½ cups (36 fl oz/1.1 l) Chicken Stock (page 106) or low-sodium chicken broth

½ cup (3 oz/90 g) diced dried apricots

½ cup (3 oz/90 g) pitted dried cherries

1 small butternut squash, about 1½ lb (750 g)

2 teaspoons olive oil

Kosher salt and freshly ground pepper

½ cup (2 oz/60 g) chopped toasted pecans

Preheat the oven to 400°F (200°C).

In a saucepan over medium-low heat, melt the butter. Add the onion and sauté until tender, about 4 minutes. Stir in the curry powder, wild rice, cinnamon stick, and orange zest. Cook, stirring, until the ingredients are well coated, about 2 minutes. Add the stock, apricots, and cherries and bring to a boil over high heat. Cover, reduce the heat to medium-low, and simmer until the rice is tender, about 55 minutes.

While the rice is cooking, halve, seed, and peel the butternut squash and then cut it into large cubes. Place the squash cubes in a single layer on a rimmed baking sheet and toss with the oil and salt and pepper to taste. Roast until the squash is tender, about 15 minutes. Keep warm. When the rice is done, remove the pan from the heat and let it stand, covered, for 10 minutes.

Transfer the rice mixture to a warmed serving bowl, discarding the cinnamon stick and orange zest. Fold in the squash and pecans. Season with to taste salt and pepper and serve right away.

Kale Salad with Quinoa

PREP TIME 25 MINUTES **SERVES** 4–6

1 teaspoon honey

1 teaspoon Dijon mustard

3 tablespoons white wine vinegar

¼ cup (2 fl oz/60 ml) extra-virgin olive oil

Kosher salt and freshly ground pepper

2 bunches Tuscan kale, stems removed and leaves julienned

½ cup (3 oz/90 g) cooked and cooled white quinoa

¼ red onion, thinly sliced

¼ cup (1 oz/30 g) coarsely chopped pistachios

¼ cup (1 oz/30 g) pomegranate seeds

In a small bowl, whisk together the honey, mustard, vinegar, oil, ½ teaspoon salt, and ¼ teaspoon pepper to make a vinaigrette.

About 30 minutes before serving, in a large bowl, combine the kale and half of the vinaigrette. Toss well and set aside.

When ready to serve, add the quinoa, red onion, pistachios, and pomegranate seeds to the bowl with the kale and toss to combine. Taste and add more vinaigrette if desired, tossing well. Season to taste with salt and pepper and serve right away.

Note: To cook quinoa, combine 1 part rinsed quinoa, 2 parts water or broth, and a pinch of kosher salt in a saucepan. Bring to a boil over high heat, then reduce the heat to low, cover, and simmer until most of the liquid has been absorbed, about 15 minutes.

Roasted Sweet Potatoes with Herbed Yogurt

PREP TIME 15 MINUTES **COOK TIME** 30 MINUTES
SERVES 8

6 small orange-fleshed sweet potatoes, about 4 lb (2 kg) total weight

6 tablespoons (3 fl oz/90 ml) olive oil

Kosher salt and freshly ground pepper

1½ cups (12 oz/375 g) plain yogurt

2 tablespoons chopped fresh flat-leaf parsley

1 tablespoon chopped fresh mint, plus small mint leaves for garnish

Calabrian chiles packed in olive oil

Preheat the oven to 425°F (220°C).

Cut the sweet potatoes lengthwise into 8 wedges each and spread on 1 or 2 rimmed baking sheets. Drizzle with the oil and sprinkle with salt and pepper. Toss to coat evenly, then spread the sweet potatoes in a single layer on the sheet(s).

Roast, turning every 10 minutes, until the sweet potatoes are evenly browned and tender, about 30 minutes.

Meanwhile, in a small bowl, stir together the yogurt, parsley, chopped mint, 1 teaspoon salt, and ¼ teaspoon pepper. Transfer the sweet potatoes to a warmed platter. Dot with the Calabrian chiles and garnish with the mint leaves. Serve right away with the yogurt sauce.

Roasted Broccoli with Pine Nuts & Parmesan

PREP TIME 10 MINUTES **COOK TIME** 35 MINUTES
SERVES 8–10

½ cup (2½ oz/75 g) pine nuts

4 lb (2 kg) broccoli

¼ cup (2 fl oz/60 ml) olive oil

Kosher salt and freshly ground pepper

2 pinches of red pepper flakes

Large chunk of Parmesan cheese

Preheat the oven to 400°F (200°C).

In a dry frying pan over medium heat, warm the pine nuts, stirring frequently, until golden brown and fragrant, about 5 minutes. Immediately pour the nuts onto a plate to cool.

Cut off the broccoli stems and reserve for another use. Separate the heads into 1-inch (2.5-cm) florets. Spread the florets on 1 or 2 large rimmed baking sheets. Drizzle with the oil and sprinkle with salt and pepper. Toss to coat evenly, then spread the florets in a single layer on the sheet(s).

Roast, turning every 10 minutes, until the broccoli florets are evenly browned and tender, about 30 minutes.

Transfer the broccoli to a warmed platter and sprinkle with the pine nuts and red pepper flakes. Using a vegetable peeler, shave the Parmesan cheese over the top. Serve right away.

Creamed Pearl Onions

PREP TIME 15 MINUTES   **COOK TIME** 20 MINUTES
SERVES 8–10

2 lb (1 kg) pearl onions or other small white boiling onions

3 tablespoons unsalted butter

3 tablespoons all-purpose flour

1¾ cups (14 fl oz/430 ml) whole milk, warmed

½ teaspoon freshly grated nutmeg

Kosher salt and freshly ground white pepper

3 tablespoons minced fresh flat-leaf parsley

Bring a saucepan filled with water to a boil over high heat. Add the onions, blanch for 2 minutes, drain, and immerse in cold water to cool. Trim the root ends, slip off the skins, then cut a small cross in the root end of each onion. Return the onions to the pan, add water just to cover, bring to a boil, reduce the heat to low, cover, and simmer gently until tender, 15–20 minutes.

Meanwhile, in a small saucepan over medium heat, melt the butter. Whisk in the flour and cook, stirring, for 1–2 minutes. Gradually whisk in the warm milk and cook, stirring constantly, until smooth and thickened, 2–3 minutes. Add the nutmeg and season to taste with salt and white pepper.

Drain the onions well and return them to the pan. Pour the sauce over the onions, stir to coat the onions well, and transfer the mixture to a warmed serving dish. Sprinkle with the parsley and serve right away.

Cauliflower Steaks with Brown Butter

PREP TIME 10 MINUTES   **COOK TIME** 20 MINUTES
SERVES 8

2 heads cauliflower

2 tablespoons olive oil

Kosher salt and freshly ground pepper

¾ cup (6 oz/185 g) unsalted butter

½ cup (4 oz/125g) capers

6 tablespoons (1 oz/30 g) chopped fresh flat-leaf parsley

2 lemons, cut into quarters

Preheat the oven to 400°F (200°C). Line 2 rimmed baking sheets with parchment paper.

Working with 1 head at a time, place the cauliflower, stem side down, on a cutting board and cut it vertically into slices ¾ inch (2 cm) thick. Place the slices in a single layer on the prepared baking sheets. Brush the slices with the oil and season with salt and pepper.

Roast until the cauliflower is tender and caramelized, about 20 minutes.

Meanwhile, in a small saucepan over medium heat, melt the butter, swirling the pan until the butter foams and begins to brown, 4–5 minutes; take care not to let the butter burn. Keep warm.

Transfer the cauliflower slices to a warmed platter. Drizzle the cauliflower with the brown butter and sprinkle with the capers and parsley. Serve right away with lemon wedges for squeezing.

Gravies & Relishes

Classic Turkey Gravy

PREP TIME 10 MINUTES   **COOK TIME** 10 MINUTES
SERVES 8–10

Drippings from one 12–18 lb (6–9 kg) roast turkey

3 tablespoons unsalted butter

3 tablespoons all-purpose flour

2 cups (16 fl oz/500 ml) Turkey Stock (page 106), Chicken Stock (page 106), or low-sodium poultry broth

1 tablespoon chicken demi-glace (optional)

2 tablespoons dry sherry (optional)

Kosher salt and freshly ground pepper

Place the roasting pan with the pan drippings on the stove top over medium-high heat. Pour in ¾ cup (6 fl oz/180 ml) water and bring to a brisk simmer, stirring with a whisk to scrape up any browned bits on the pan bottom. Simmer until the liquid is slightly reduced, about 1 minute. Carefully strain the contents of the pan through a fine-mesh sieve into a heatproof bowl or a fat separator and set aside. If the drippings are in a bowl, spoon off as much fat from them as possible.

In a saucepan pan over medium heat, melt the butter. When it bubbles, add the flour and cook, whisking constantly, until the flour is golden brown, 2–3 minutes. Slowly whisk in the degreased drippings from the bowl or from the fat separator, leaving the fat behind in the separator, if using. Whisk in the stock and the demi-glace, if desired, and cook, stirring constantly, until the gravy is smooth and thick enough to coat the back of a spoon 2–3 minutes. Stir in the sherry, if desired, and season with salt and pepper.

Pour the gravy into a warmed gravy boat for serving.

Gluten-Free Brown Gravy

PREP TIME 10 MINUTES   **COOK TIME** 10 MINUTES
SERVES 10–12

Drippings from one 12–18 lb (6–9 kg) roast turkey

6 tablespoons (3 oz/90 g) unsalted butter

1 shallot, minced

½ cup (3 oz/90 g) fine rice flour

6 cups (48 fl oz/1.5 l) Turkey Stock (page 106), Chicken Stock (page 106), or low-sodium poultry broth

Kosher salt and freshly ground pepper

1 fresh thyme sprig

1 fresh rosemary sprig

1 bay leaf

Place the roasting pan with the pan drippings on the stove top over medium-high heat. Pour in ¾ cup (6 fl oz/180 ml) water and bring to a brisk simmer, stirring with a whisk to scrape up any browned bits on the pan bottom. Simmer until the liquid is slightly reduced, about 1 minute. Carefully strain the contents of the pan through a fine-mesh sieve into a heatproof bowl or a fat separator and set aside. If the drippings are in a bowl, spoon off as much fat from them as possible.

In a saucepan over medium heat, melt the butter. Add the shallot and sauté until translucent, about 2 minutes. Whisk in the rice flour and cook, whisking constantly, until golden brown, 4–5 minutes. Slowly whisk in the degreased drippings from the bowl or from the fat separator, leaving the fat behind in the separator, if using. Whisk in the stock. Bring to a simmer, whisking constantly. Season with salt and pepper. Add the thyme, rosemary, and bay leaf.

Remove the pan from the heat and let the gravy stand for 5 minutes to infuse the herb flavors. Discard the herbs and pour the gravy into a warmed gravy boat for serving.

Madeira-Sage Gravy

PREP TIME 15 MINUTES   **COOK TIME** 25 MINUTES
SERVES 8–10

Drippings from one 12–18 lb (6–9 kg) roast turkey

1 cup (8 fl oz/250 ml) Madeira

6 tablespoons (3 fl oz/90 ml) canola oil

1 lb (500 g) shallots, halved lengthwise

⅓ cup (2 oz/60 g) all-purpose flour

4 cups (32 fl oz/1 l) Turkey Stock (page 106), Chicken Stock (page 106), or low-sodium poultry broth

2 bay leaves

4 large fresh sage sprigs

Kosher salt and freshly ground pepper

Place the roasting pan with the pan drippings on the stove top over medium-high heat. Pour in the Madeira and bring to a brisk simmer, stirring with a whisk to scrape up any browned bits on the pan bottom. Simmer until the liquid is slightly reduced, about 1 minute. Carefully strain the contents of the pan through a fine-mesh sieve into a heatproof bowl or a fat separator and set aside.

In a large sauté pan over medium heat, warm the oil. Add the shallots and sauté until browned, 10–15 minutes. Add the flour and cook, stirring constantly, until fragrant, about 1 minute.

Slowly whisk in the stock and add the bay leaves and sage sprigs. Raise the heat to medium-high and bring to a simmer, then reduce the heat to medium-low and simmer, whisking occasionally, until thickened, 8–10 minutes.

Remove from the heat, strain through the fine-mesh sieve into a clean saucepan, and discard the solids. If the strained drippings are in a bowl, spoon off as much fat from them as possible, then pour the drippings into the saucepan. If using a fat separator, pour the drippings into the saucepan, leaving the fat behind in the separator. Stir well, then heat the gravy over medium heat until hot. Season with salt and pepper.

Pour the gravy into a warmed gravy boat for serving.

Giblet Gravy

PREP TIME 15 MINUTES   **COOK TIME** 15 MINUTES
SERVES 10–12

Drippings from one 12–18 lb (6–9 kg) roast turkey

7 cups (56 fl oz/1.75 l) Turkey Stock (page 106), Chicken Stock (page 106), or low-sodium poultry broth

Reserved cooked neck, heart, and gizzard from the roast turkey

¼ cup (1 oz/30 g) cornstarch

Kosher salt and freshly ground pepper

Place the roasting pan with the pan drippings on the stove top over medium-high heat. Pour in all but ¼ cup (2 fl oz/60 ml) of the stock and bring to a brisk simmer, stirring with a whisk to scrape up any browned bits on the pan bottom. Simmer for about 5 minutes.

Carefully strain the contents of the pan through a fine-mesh sieve into a heatproof bowl or a fat separator. If the drippings are in a bowl, spoon off as much fat from them as possible, then pour the liquid into a wide saucepan. If the drippings are in a fat separator, pour the liquid into a wide saucepan, leaving the fat behind in the separator. Place the saucepan over medium-high heat and simmer briskly for 5 minutes to reduce slightly.

Meanwhile, remove the meat from the turkey neck, then finely chop the neck meat, heart, and gizzard. When the liquid has simmered for 5 minutes, add the chopped giblets and reduce the heat to low. In a small bowl, stir together the cornstarch and the remaining ¼ cup (2 fl oz/60 ml) stock to make a paste. Gradually stir the paste into the simmering liquid and cook, stirring, until the gravy thickens, 3–4 minutes. Season with salt and pepper.

Pour the gravy into a warmed gravy boat for serving.

Herbed Citrus Gravy

PREP TIME 15 MINUTES **COOK TIME** 15 MINUTES
SERVES 10–12

7 cups (56 fl oz/1.75 l) Turkey Stock (page 106), Chicken Stock (page 106), or low-sodium poultry broth

¼ cup (1 oz/30 g) cornstarch

½ cup (¾ oz/20 g) minced fresh flat-leaf parsley

1 tablespoon finely grated lemon zest

1 tablespoon fresh lemon juice

Kosher salt and freshly ground pepper

Pour all but ¼ cup (2 fl oz/60 ml) of the stock into a wide saucepan and place over medium-high heat. Bring to a simmer and simmer briskly for 10 minutes.

In a small bowl, stir together the cornstarch and the remaining ¼ cup (2 fl oz/60 ml) stock to make a paste. Gradually stir the paste into the simmering liquid, then add the parsley, lemon zest, and lemon juice. Cook, stirring, until the gravy thickens, 3–4 minutes. Season with salt and pepper.

Pour the gravy into a warmed gravy boat for serving.

Note: You may vary the herbs according to your preference; thyme, sage, and tarragon, or a combination, also work well. This is a good gravy to make as a backup, as you don't need turkey drippings as a base. Use Vegetable Stock (page 106) to make this a vegetarian gravy.

Port Gravy

PREP TIME 25 MINUTES **INACTIVE PREP TIME** 8 HOURS
COOK TIME 2¼ HOURS **SERVES** 8–10

5 tablespoons (2½ oz/75 g) unsalted butter

Neck, heart, and gizzard reserved from a 12–18 lb (6–9 kg) turkey, coarsely chopped

1 carrot, peeled and coarsely chopped

1 yellow onion, coarsely chopped

1 rib celery, coarsely chopped

1 head garlic, halved crosswise

1 fresh thyme sprig

1 cup (8 fl oz/250 ml) dry white wine

2 cups (16 fl oz/500 ml) ruby port

4 cups (32 fl oz/1 l) Turkey Stock (page 106), Chicken Stock (page 106), or low-sodium poultry broth

¼ cup (1½ oz/45 g) all-purpose flour

¾ cup (6 fl oz/180 ml) heavy cream

In a large saucepan over high heat, melt 1 tablespoon of the butter. Add the turkey giblets, carrot, onion, and celery and cook, stirring often, until dark golden brown but not scorched, 8–10 minutes. Add the garlic, thyme, white wine, and port and bring to a boil, stirring with a wooden spoon to scrape up any browned bits on the pan bottom. Add the stock, bring to a boil, and reduce the heat to maintain a gentle simmer. Simmer until reduced and very flavorful, about 1½ hours, skimming off any foam and fat from the surface of the liquid every 20 minutes with a large, shallow metal spoon.

Strain the liquid through a fine-mesh sieve into a large saucepan, pressing down on the solids with the back of a spoon. Place over medium-high heat and simmer briskly until reduced by about half, again skimming off any fat if necessary. Transfer to a glass container, then cool, cover, and refrigerate overnight.

While the turkey roasts, finish the gravy: Lift off and discard any fat from the surface of the chilled stock. In a large, clean saucepan over medium-low heat, melt the remaining 4 tablespoons (2 oz/60 g) butter and stir in the flour. Cook, stirring constantly with a whisk, until light brown, about 3 minutes. Gradually whisk in the stock and bring to a simmer. Cook gently, uncovered, for about 30 minutes. Whisk in the cream, return to a brisk simmer, and cook for 2 minutes.

Pour the gravy into a warmed gravy boat for serving.

Cranberry Compote with Riesling & Pears

PREP TIME 10 MINUTES   **COOK TIME** 25 MINUTES
SERVES 8–10

2 tablespoons unsalted butter

2 Anjou pears, peeled, cored, and diced

4 cups (1 lb/500 g) fresh or thawed frozen cranberries

2 cups (16 fl oz/500 ml) Riesling

½ cup (3½ oz/105 g) firmly packed golden brown sugar

Pinch of cayenne pepper

4 thin strips lemon zest

1 cinnamon stick

2 star anise pods

8 cloves

In a 4-quart (4-l) saucepan over medium-high heat, melt the butter. Add the pears and cook, stirring occasionally, until they are starting to brown, 8–10 minutes. Add the cranberries, wine, brown sugar, cayenne, and lemon zest. Tie the cinnamon stick, star anise, and cloves in a square of cheesecloth and add the sachet to the pan. Bring to a simmer, then reduce the heat to medium and cook, stirring occasionally, until the compote has thickened and the cranberries have begun to burst, 15–20 minutes. Remove the pan from the heat.

Remove and discard the spice sachet. Taste the compote and add more brown sugar, if desired. Serve warm, cold, or at room temperature.

Port-Spiked Cranberry Sauce

PREP TIME 10 MINUTES   **COOK TIME** 20 MINUTES
SERVES 10–12

1 cup (8 fl oz/250 ml) ruby port

4 cups (1 lb/500 g) fresh cranberries

1 cup (8 oz/250 g) sugar

Finely grated zest of 1 orange

1 cup (8 fl oz/250 ml) fresh orange juice

Finely grated zest of 1 lemon

1 cinnamon stick

In a large saucepan over medium-high heat, simmer the port until reduced by half, about 5 minutes. Add the cranberries, sugar, orange zest, orange juice, lemon zest, and cinnamon stick. Bring to a simmer, stirring occasionally, then reduce the heat to medium-low and simmer until the cranberries have burst and the juices have reduced and are thick enough to coat the back of a spoon, about 15 minutes.

Let the sauce cool to room temperature, then cover and refrigerate until ready to serve.

Discard the cinnamon stick and bring the sauce to room temperature before serving.

Cranberry-Orange Relish

PREP TIME 10 MINUTES **INACTIVE PREP TIME** 24 HOURS
SERVES 8–10

1 orange

2 bags (12 oz/375 g each) fresh cranberries

1½ cups (12 oz/375 g) sugar

⅓ cup (2 oz/60 g) peeled and finely chopped fresh ginger

Cut the orange (with its peel on) into 16 chunks and discard any seeds. Working in batches, combine the orange chunks, cranberries, sugar, and ginger in a food processor. Pulse to chop finely and evenly, stopping once or twice with each batch to scrape down the sides of the work bowl.

Transfer to a storage container, cover, and refrigerate for at least 24 hours or up to 3 days to develop the flavors. Bring to room temperature and stir well before serving.

Sweet Onion Marmalade

PREP TIME 10 MINUTES **COOK TIME** 1 HOUR
SERVES 8–10

¼ cup (2 fl oz/60 ml) extra-virgin olive oil

6 Vidalia or other sweet onions, about 3 lb (1.5 kg) total weight, coarsely chopped

¾ teaspoon kosher salt

¼ cup (2 oz/60 g) firmly packed golden brown sugar

¼ cup (2 fl oz/60 ml) white balsamic vinegar

3 tablespoons white wine vinegar

1 tablespoon honey

1 teaspoon dried thyme

Freshly ground pepper

In a large frying pan over medium heat, warm the oil. Add the onions and salt and stir to coat the onions with the oil. Cover and cook, stirring occasionally, until the onions are soft and pale gold, about 30 minutes.

Stir in the brown sugar, vinegars, honey, and thyme. Season to taste with pepper. Simmer uncovered, stirring occasionally, until the onion juices have evaporated and the mixture is thick, about 30 minutes.

Let the mixture cool to room temperature for immediate use, or transfer to an airtight container, cover, and refrigerate for up to 3 weeks before serving.

Horseradish–Apple Sauce

PREP TIME 10 MINUTES **SERVES** 12–15

1 red apple

2 cups (16 oz/500 g) prepared cream-style horseradish

½ cup (4 oz/125 g) sour cream

½ cup (4 fl oz/125 ml) mayonnaise

1 tablespoon chopped fresh chives

1 teaspoon sugar

Freshly ground pepper

Using the large holes on a box grater-shredder, coarsely grate the apple flesh, avoiding the core.

In a bowl, stir together the horseradish, sour cream, and mayonnaise. Add the grated apple, chives, and sugar and stir until well mixed. Season to taste with pepper.

Cover tightly and refrigerate until ready to serve or for up to 4 days. Serve cold.

Citrus & Mint Compote

PREP TIME 15 MINUTES **INACTIVE PREP TIME** 30 MINUTES

SERVES 8–10

12 large blood oranges or navel oranges

¼ cup (2 fl oz/60 ml) crème de cassis

2 tablespoons fresh lemon juice

3 tablespoons minced fresh mint

1 tablespoon grated orange zest

Pomegranate seeds for garnish (optional)

Working with 1 orange at a time, cut a slice off the top and bottom to reveal the flesh. Stand the fruit upright. Using a sharp knife, thickly slice away the peel and pith, cutting downward and following the natural contour of the fruit. Holding the fruit over a bowl, cut along either side of each section of flesh, freeing it from its membrane and dropping the flesh into the bowl. Repeat this process with the remaining oranges.

Pour the cassis and lemon juice over the oranges and stir to blend. Cover and refrigerate for 30–60 minutes.

To serve, transfer the oranges to a serving dish and sprinkle with the mint, orange zest, and the pomegranate seeds, if using.

Desserts

Classic Pumpkin Pie

PREP TIME 1 HOUR **INACTIVE PREP TIME** 4½ HOURS
COOK TIME 1¾ HOURS **SERVES** 10

1 recipe Basic Pie Dough
for a double-crust pie
(page 107), shaped into
2 disks and chilled

1 large egg, lightly beaten
with 1 tablespoon water

FOR THE FILLING
1¼ cups (9 oz/280 g) firmly
packed golden brown sugar

1 tablespoon cornstarch

½ teaspoon kosher salt

1½ teaspoons ground
cinnamon

½ teaspoon ground ginger

¼ teaspoon freshly grated
nutmeg

⅛ teaspoon ground cloves

2 cups (19 oz/590 g) canned
pumpkin purée

3 large eggs, lightly beaten

1 cup (8 fl oz/250 ml) heavy
cream

⅓ cup (3 fl oz/80 ml) whole
milk

Remove the dough disks from the refrigerator and let stand at
room temperature for 5 minutes. Unwrap 1 dough disk and place
it on a lightly floured work surface. Roll out the dough into a
12-inch (30-cm) round. Transfer the dough round to a 9-inch
(23-cm) deep-dish pie dish. Using a paring knife, trim the dough
edges, leaving a ½-inch (12-mm) overhang. Fold the overhang
under itself around the rim of the dish and flute the dough edges,
if desired.

Roll out the remaining dough disk. Using decorative pastry
cutters or a paring knife, cut out shapes from the second dough
round. Transfer the shapes to a parchment paper–lined baking
sheet. Refrigerate the pie shell and the cutouts for 30 minutes.

Position a rack in the lower third of the oven, place a rimmed
baking sheet in the oven, and preheat to 400°F (200°C).

Brush the edges of the pie shell with some of the egg wash. Line
the pie shell with parchment paper and fill with pie weights. Place
on the preheated baking sheet and bake for 20 minutes. Remove
the weights and parchment and continue to bake until the pie
shell is golden, about 5 minutes more. Let cool on a wire rack.

Reduce the oven temperature to 375°F (190°C).

Brush the dough cutouts with the egg mixture and bake until
golden, 15–20 minutes. Let cool on a wire rack.

To make the filling, in a bowl, combine the brown sugar,
cornstarch, salt, cinnamon, ginger, nutmeg, and cloves and
whisk to mix. Whisk in the pumpkin, eggs, cream, and milk
until blended.

Pour the filling into the cooled pie shell and bake until the
filling is set, 60–65 minutes. If the edges of the crust are
browning too quickly, cover them with strips of aluminum
foil. Transfer the pie to a wire rack and let cool for at least
2 hours before serving.

Arrange the dough cutouts decoratively on top of the pie just
before serving.

Chocolate Ganache Tart

PREP TIME 20 MINUTES   **INACTIVE PREP TIME** 2¼ HOURS

COOK TIME 35 MINUTES   **SERVES** 8–10

1 large egg yolk

2 tablespoons plus
1 teaspoon ice water

3 teaspoons pure vanilla
extract

1¼ cups (6½ oz/200 g)
all-purpose flour

⅓ cup (3 oz/90 g) sugar

¼ cup (¾ oz/20 g)
unsweetened cocoa powder

¼ teaspoon kosher salt

⅔ cup (5 oz/155 g) cold
unsalted butter

10 oz (315 g) semisweet
or bittersweet chocolate,
chopped

1 cup (8 fl oz/250 ml)
heavy cream

Fleur de sel sea salt

In a bowl, stir together the egg yolk, ice water, and 2 teaspoons of the vanilla.

In a stand mixer fitted with the paddle attachment, combine the flour, sugar, cocoa powder, and kosher salt and mix briefly on low speed to mix. Add ½ cup (4 oz/125 g) of the butter and beat on medium-low speed until the mixture resembles coarse cornmeal. Add the egg mixture and beat until the dough comes together. Remove the dough from the mixer, shape it into a disk, wrap it in plastic wrap, and refrigerate for 1 hour.

Preheat the oven to 350°F (180°C). On a lightly floured work surface, roll out the dough to fit a 4-by-13-inch (10-by-33-cm) rectangular tart pan with a removable bottom. Press the dough into the bottom and up the sides of the pan. Using a paring knife, cut off the dough overhang. Using a fork, prick the dough all over.

Line the dough with parchment paper and fill with pie weights. Bake for 25 minutes. Remove the weights and parchment and continue to bake until the bottom is dry, about 8 minutes more. Let cool on a wire rack.

In a heatproof bowl, combine the chocolate and the remaining 2 tablespoons butter. In a saucepan over medium-high heat, bring the cream just to a boil. Pour the hot cream over the chocolate. Let stand for 2 minutes, then add the remaining 1 teaspoon vanilla and whisk until smooth to make a ganache.

Pour the ganache into the tart shell. Sprinkle to taste with fleur de sel and refrigerate until the filling is set, about 1 hour. Remove from the refrigerator 15 minutes before serving.

Red Wine–Poached Pears

PREP TIME 15 MINUTES   **COOK TIME** 25 MINUTES

SERVES 8

¼ cup (2¼ oz/70 g) mulling
spices

4 firm but ripe Bosc pears
with stems intact

2 cups (16 fl oz/500 ml)
full-bodied red wine, such
as Zinfandel or Cabernet
Sauvignon

½ cup (4 fl oz/125 ml) fresh
orange juice

⅓ cup (3 oz/90 g) sugar

1 cup (8 oz/250 g)
mascarpone cheese

1 tablespoon honey

1 teaspoon finely grated
orange zest

1 cup (3 oz/90 g) assorted
dried fruits, such as figs,
cherries, and cranberries

Put the mulling spices in a stainless-steel spice ball or tie them in a square of cheesecloth. Cut a round of parchment paper to fit the diameter of a saucepan; set the paper aside.

Using a vegetable peeler, peel the pears almost to the top. In the saucepan over medium heat, combine the wine, orange juice, sugar, pears, spice ball, and 1½ cups (12 fl oz/375 ml) water. Bring to a boil, stirring occasionally, then reduce the heat to low. Press the parchment round directly onto the pears and liquid. Cover and simmer until the pears are tender, 15–20 minutes.

While the pears are poaching, in a bowl, stir together the mascarpone, honey, and orange zest. Set aside.

When the pears are ready, remove them from the pan using a slotted spoon. Add the dried fruits to the poaching liquid and simmer over low heat until the fruits are plump and tender, 5–10 minutes. Using a slotted spoon, remove the fruits from the pan and raise the heat to medium-high. Bring the liquid to a boil and cook until slightly reduced, 1–2 minutes.

Cut the pears in half lengthwise and scoop out the core with a melon baller.

To serve, spread an equal amount of the mascarpone mixture on each of 8 small plates. Top with the pear halves and dried fruits and drizzle with the reduced poaching liquid.

Apple-Cranberry Pie

PREP TIME 40 MINUTES   INACTIVE PREP TIME 3½ HOURS
COOK TIME 1 HOUR   SERVES 8

1 recipe Basic Pie Dough
for a double-crust pie
(page 107), shaped
into 2 disks and chilled

4 lb (2 kg) Golden Delicious
apples, peeled, halved,
cored, and thinly sliced

1½ cups (6 oz/185 g) fresh
cranberries

¼ cup (1½ oz/45 g) chopped
crystallized ginger

¾ cup (6 oz/185 g) sugar

¼ teaspoon kosher salt

3 tablespoons all-purpose
flour

1 tablespoon fresh lemon
juice

1 large egg, lightly beaten
with 1 teaspoon water

Vanilla ice cream for serving
(optional)

Remove the dough disks from the refrigerator and let stand
at room temperature for 5 minutes. Unwrap 1 dough disk and
place it on a lightly floured work surface. Roll out the dough
into a 12-inch (30-cm) round. Transfer the dough round to a
9-inch (23-cm) deep-dish pie dish. Using a paring knife, trim
the dough edges, leaving a ½-inch (12-mm) overhang. Reroll the
dough scraps and cut out shapes using decorative pastry cutters.
Roll out the second dough disk as you did the first. Refrigerate
the pie shell, dough round, and cutouts for 30 minutes.

Position a rack in the lower third of the oven and preheat to
400°F (200°C).

In a large bowl, toss together the apples, cranberries, ginger,
sugar, salt, flour, and lemon juice.

Let the pie shell, dough round, and cutouts stand at room
temperature for 5 minutes. Pour the apple filling into the pie
shell and carefully transfer the dough round over the filling. Trim
the edges flush with the rim and press the top and bottom crusts
together. Flute the dough edges, if desired. Brush the underside
of the cutouts with the egg wash and arrange them on the pie.
Using a small, sharp knife, cut 4 vents into the top crust. Brush
the entire top crust with the egg wash and sprinkle with sugar.

Bake the pie until the crust is golden and the filling is bubbling,
about 1 hour, covering the edges of the crust with strips of
aluminum foil if they begin to brown too quickly. Transfer
to a wire rack and let cool for 1 hour before serving.

Cut the pie into wedges and serve with ice cream, if desired.

Apple Crumb Pie

PREP TIME 40 MINUTES   INACTIVE PREP TIME 3½ HOURS
COOK TIME 50 MINUTES   SERVES 8

1 recipe Basic Pie Dough
for a single-crust pie
(page 107), shaped into
1 disk and chilled

FOR THE TOPPING

½ cup (2½ oz/75 g)
all-purpose flour

⅓ cup (2½ oz/75 g) firmly
packed golden brown sugar

1 teaspoon ground cinnamon

¼ teaspoon kosher salt

5 tablespoons (2½ oz/75 g)
cold unsalted butter, cut
into cubes

FOR THE FILLING

7 large, tart, firm apples,
peeled, cored, and diced

1 tablespoon fresh lemon
juice

⅓ cup (3 oz/90 g)
granulated sugar

2 tablespoons cornstarch

1 teaspoon ground cinnamon

½ teaspoon freshly grated
nutmeg

¼ teaspoon ground cloves

Pinch of kosher salt

Remove the dough disk from the refrigerator and let stand at
room temperature for 5 minutes. Unwrap the dough and place
it on a lightly floured work surface. Roll out the dough into a
12-inch (30-cm) round. Transfer the dough round to a 9-inch
(23-cm) pie pan or dish. Using a paring knife, trim the dough
edges, leaving a ½-inch (12-mm) overhang. Fold the dough
under itself to form a rim and flute the edges decoratively.

To make the topping, in a small bowl, stir together the flour,
brown sugar, cinnamon, and salt. Scatter the butter over the
top and, using a pastry blender or 2 knives, cut in the butter
until the mixture is crumbly. Cover and refrigerate until ready
to use.

To make the filling, place the apples in a large bowl, sprinkle
with the lemon juice, and toss to coat evenly. In a small bowl,
stir together the granulated sugar, cornstarch, cinnamon,
nutmeg, cloves, and salt. Sprinkle the sugar mixture over the
apples and toss to distribute evenly. Immediately transfer to
the dough-lined pan. Sprinkle evenly with the topping.

Refrigerate the pie until the dough is firm, 20–30 minutes.
Meanwhile, position a rack in the lower third of the oven and
preheat to 375°F (190°C).

Bake the pie until the crust is golden and the filling is thick and
bubbling, 50–60 minutes. Transfer to a wire rack and let cool
completely to set. Serve at room temperature or rewarm in a
350°F (180°C) oven for 10–15 minutes just before serving.

Bite-Sized Pecan Tartlets

PREP TIME 35 MINUTES **INACTIVE PREP TIME** 2¾ HOURS
COOK TIME 35 MINUTES **MAKES** 36 TARTLETS

1 recipe Basic Pie Dough for a double-crust pie (page 107), shaped into 2 disks and chilled

1½ cups (6 oz/185 g) coarsely chopped pecans

3 large eggs

¾ cup (7½ oz/235 g) dark corn syrup

⅔ cup (5 oz/155 g) firmly packed dark brown sugar

¼ cup (3 oz/90 g) light molasses

4 tablespoons (2 oz/60 g) unsalted butter, melted and slightly cooled

1 tablespoon Kahlúa or other coffee-flavored liqueur

½ teaspoon kosher salt

Whipped cream for serving (optional)

Let 1 chilled dough disk stand at room temperature for 5 minutes. Place the dough on a lightly floured work surface. Roll out into a 12-inch (30-cm) round about ⅛ inch (3 mm) thick. Using a fluted or plain 2½-inch (6-cm) biscuit cutter, cut out 18 rounds. (If necessary, reroll the dough scraps to yield 18 rounds, rerolling and chilling the dough scraps as needed.)

Position a rack in the lower third of the oven and preheat to 325°F (165°C). Lightly spray 36 mini muffin cups with nonstick cooking spray. Ease each round into a prepared muffin cup, gently pressing it against the bottom and up the sides of the cup. Refrigerate for at least 30 minutes before filling. Repeat with the remaining dough disk and muffin cups.

Toast the pecans in a shallow pan in the oven, stirring once or twice, until lightly browned, 8–10 minutes. Let cool. Raise the oven temperature to 375°F (190°C).

In a large bowl, whisk the eggs until blended. Add the corn syrup, brown sugar, molasses, butter, liqueur, and salt and whisk until smooth. Place about 2 teaspoons of the pecans in each chilled tartlet shell. Pour about 1 tablespoon of the egg mixture over the pecans, filling the cup to within ⅛ inch (3 mm) of the rim.

Bake until the pastry has browned edges and the filling is evenly but not firmly set, about 25 minutes. Let cool in the pans on wire racks for 5–10 minutes, then use a small spoon to ease each one out of its cup to cool completely on a wire rack. Serve with whipped cream, if desired, or store in an airtight container at room temperature for up to 3 days.

Pecan Pie

PREP TIME 45 MINUTES **INACTIVE PREP TIME** 4 HOURS
COOK TIME 50 MINUTES **SERVES** 8

1 recipe Basic Pie Dough for a single-crust pie (page 107), shaped into 1 disk and chilled

3 large eggs

¾ cup (7½ oz/235 g) dark corn syrup

⅔ cup (5 oz/155 g) firmly packed dark brown sugar

¼ cup (3 oz/90 g) light molasses

4 tablespoons (2 oz/60 g) unsalted butter, melted and slightly cooled

1 tablespoon Kahlúa or other coffee-flavored liqueur

¼ teaspoon kosher salt

1½ cups (6 oz/185 g) halved pecans

Whipped cream for serving (optional)

Remove the dough disk from the refrigerator and let stand at room temperature for 5 minutes. Unwrap the dough and place it on a lightly floured work surface. Roll out the dough into a 12-inch (30-cm) round. Transfer the dough round to a 9-inch (23-cm) pie pan or dish. Using a paring knife, trim the dough edges, leaving a ½-inch (12-mm) overhang. Fold the dough under itself to form a rim and flute the edges decoratively.

Position a rack in the lower third of the oven and preheat to 350°F (180°C). In a large bowl, whisk the eggs until well blended. Add the corn syrup, brown sugar, molasses, butter, liqueur, and salt and whisk until smooth.

Scatter the pecans evenly in the pie shell. Pour the egg mixture over the pecans.

Bake the pie until the top is browned and the filling is evenly but not firmly set, about 50 minutes. Check the pie after 40 minutes and cover the edges of the crust with strips of aluminum foil if they are browning too quickly. Transfer the pie to a wire rack and let cool completely before cutting, about 2 hours.

To serve, cut into wedges and top each wedge with a dollop of whipped cream, if desired.

Note: This pie is good warm, but it is so soft right after baking that it is difficult to slice. If you want to serve warm slices, let the pie cool completely, cut it, then rewarm the individual slices in a 300°F (150°C) oven for 5–10 minutes just before serving.

Pumpkin Cheesecake

PREP TIME 25 MINUTES **INACTIVE PREP TIME** 8¾ HOURS
COOK TIME 40 MINUTES **SERVES** 10–12

FOR THE CRUST

4 oz (125 g) gingersnaps (about 20 small cookies)

⅓ cup (1½ oz/45 g) pecan halves

¼ cup (2 oz/60 g) firmly packed golden brown sugar

4 tablespoons (2 oz/60 g) unsalted butter, melted

¾ cup (6 oz/185 g) firmly packed golden brown sugar

1 teaspoon ground cinnamon

¼ teaspoon ground allspice

¼ teaspoon ground ginger

¼ teaspoon ground cloves

1 lb (500 g) cream cheese, at room temperature

3 large eggs

1 cup (9½ oz/295 g) canned pumpkin purée

1 tablespoon unsalted butter

½ cup (2 oz/60 g) pecan halves, coarsely chopped

2 tablespoons granulated sugar

To make the crust, in a food processor, combine the cookies and pecans and process until crumbly. Add the brown sugar and melted butter and pulse for a few seconds to blend. Transfer the crumb mixture to the prepared springform pan. Use your fingers to pat the mixture onto the bottom and evenly all the way up the sides of the pan. Refrigerate for 30 minutes.

Preheat the oven to 350°F (180°C) Lightly butter a 9-inch (23-cm) springform pan.

In a small bowl, stir together the brown sugar, cinnamon, allspice, ginger, and cloves. In a large bowl, using an electric mixer on medium speed, beat the cream cheese until smooth and creamy, scraping down the sides of the bowl occasionally. Gradually add the brown sugar mixture, beating until smooth. Beat in the eggs one at a time, beating well after each addition. Add the pumpkin purée and beat until smooth. Scrape the batter into the chilled crust and smooth the top.

Bake the cheesecake until a knife inserted into the center comes out clean, 35–40 minutes. Let cool completely on a wire rack. Cover and refrigerate for at least 8 hours or for up to 24 hours.

In a small frying pan over medium-high heat, melt the butter. Add the pecans, sprinkle with the granulated sugar, and cook, stirring, until the sugar melts and the nuts are toasted and caramel coated. Transfer the nut mixture to a plate and let cool completely. Store in an airtight container until ready to serve.

Just before serving, sprinkle the pecans over the cheesecake.

Warm Gingerbread with Brandy Sauce

PREP TIME 30 MINUTES **INACTIVE PREP TIME** 25 MINUTES
COOK TIME 30 MINUTES **SERVES** 8–10

6 tablespoons (3 oz/90 g) unsalted butter, melted

½ cup (6 oz/185 g) honey

½ cup (5½ oz/170 g) light molasses

½ cup (4 oz/125 g) sour cream

1 large egg

2 cups (10 oz/315 g) all-purpose flour

1½ teaspoons baking soda

1 teaspoon ground ginger

½ teaspoon dry mustard

½ teaspoon allspice

¼ teaspoon ground cinnamon

¼ teaspoon kosher salt

FOR THE BRANDY SAUCE

1¼ cups (5 oz/150 g) confectioners' sugar

¼ cup (2 oz/60 g) crème fraîche

¼ cup (2 fl oz/60 ml) brandy

¾ cup (6 fl oz/180 ml) heavy cream

Preheat the oven to 375°F (190°C). Butter a 9-inch (23-cm) round cake pan or springform pan with 2-inch (5-cm) sides. Dust the pan with flour and tap out the excess.

In a large bowl, stir together the butter, honey, and molasses. Add the sour cream and egg and beat until smooth. In a medium bowl, stir together the flour, baking soda, ginger, mustard, allspice, and cinnamon. Fold the flour mixture into the butter mixture and stir until blended. Scrape the batter into the prepared pan, spreading it evenly with a rubber spatula.

Bake the gingerbread until a toothpick inserted into the center comes out clean, 30–35 minutes. Transfer to a wire rack and let cool for 5 minutes. If using a round cake pan, invert the pan onto the rack, and turn the cake right side up to cool for 20–30 minutes. If using a springform pan, let the cake cool in the pan on a wire rack for 5 minutes before releasing the pan side; then cool for 20–30 minutes.

While the gingerbread is baking, make the brandy sauce: In a bowl, whisk together the confectioners' sugar, crème fraîche, and brandy until smooth. In another bowl, whip the cream until soft peaks form. Fold the cream into the sugar mixture. Cover and refrigerate until serving or for up to 6 hours. If needed, whisk again to blend before serving.

Cut the warm gingerbread into wedges and serve topped with the brandy sauce.

Boozy Ice Cream

PREP TIME 15 MINUTES **INACTIVE PREP TIME** 10½ HOURS
COOK TIME 10 MINUTES **MAKES** 1½ QUARTS (1.5 L)

4 large egg yolks

⅔ cup (5 oz/155 g) sugar

½ teaspoon freshly grated
nutmeg

2½ cups (20 fl oz/625 ml)
half-and-half

1½ cups (12 fl oz/375 ml)
heavy cream

1 teaspoon pure vanilla
extract

2 tablespoons dark rum

2 tablespoons brandy

In a bowl, whisk together the egg yolks, sugar, and nutmeg. In a heavy saucepan over medium heat, combine the half-and-half and cream and bring to a gentle simmer. Slowly whisk the hot cream mixture into the egg yolk mixture.

Return the mixture to the pan and place over low heat. Cook, stirring constantly, until the mixture thickens enough to coat the back of a metal spoon and leaves a clear track when a finger is drawn through it, about 4 minutes. Do not let the mixture boil.

Immediately transfer to a bowl and let cool to room temperature. Stir in the vanilla. Cover the bowl with plastic wrap, pressing it directly onto the surface of the custard to prevent a skin from forming. Refrigerate for at least 2 hours or preferably overnight.

Freeze in an ice-cream maker according to the manufacturer's instructions until softly frozen. Add the rum and brandy and continue to churn until the ice cream freezes further. (Due to the alcohol content, it may not freeze solid.) Transfer the ice cream to a freezer-safe container, cover, and place in the freezer overnight before serving.

Cranberry Sorbet

PREP TIME 10 MINUTES **INACTIVE PREP TIME** 5½ HOURS
COOK TIME 2 MINUTES **MAKES** 1 QUART (1 L)

1½ cups (12 oz/375 g) sugar

2½ cups (20 fl oz/625 ml)
unsweetened cranberry
juice

In a heavy saucepan over medium-high heat, combine the sugar and 1½ cups (12 fl oz/375 ml) water and bring to a boil, stirring to dissolve the sugar. Boil, stirring occasionally, until the sugar is fully dissolved.

Pour the cranberry juice into the sugar syrup and bring to a boil over medium-high heat. Reduce the heat to medium and cook for about 1 minute. Remove from the heat and set aside to cool to room temperature.

Refrigerate the cranberry syrup until chilled, at least 3 hours or for up to 8 hours.

Pour the cranberry syrup into an ice-cream maker and freeze according to the manufacturer's instructions. Transfer the sorbet to a freezer-safe container, cover, and freeze until firm, at least 2 hours or for up to 3 days, before serving.

Leftovers

Turkey, Onion & Cheddar Panini 92

Turkey Panini with Blue Cheese & Chutney 92

Turkey Banh Mi 95

Turkey with All the Trimmings Sandwich 95

Turkey, Onion & Cheddar Panini

PREP TIME 10 MINUTES **COOK TIME** 5 MINUTES
SERVES 2

4 slices coarse country
bread

Olive oil

½ cup (5 oz/155 g) Sweet
Onion Marmalade (page 76)

About 6 oz (185 g) sliced
roasted turkey

4 slices crisply cooked
bacon (optional)

4 slices sharp Cheddar
cheese

Preheat a panini maker according to the manufacturer's
instructions.

Brush 1 side of each bread slice with oil, then place the
slices, oiled side down, on a work surface. Spread the onion
marmalade on the bread slices, dividing it evenly. Divide
the turkey between 2 slices of the bread, arranging it on the
marmalade. Top the turkey with the bacon, if using, and cheese
slices, dividing them evenly. Place the remaining bread slices on
top, marmalade side down.

Place the sandwiches in the panini maker, close the top plate,
and cook until the bread is golden and toasted, the fillings
are warm, and the cheese is melted, 3–5 minutes.

Cut each sandwich in half and serve right away.

Turkey Panini with Blue Cheese & Chutney

PREP TIME 10 MINUTES **COOK TIME** 5 MINUTES
SERVES 2

4 slices coarse country
bread

Olive oil

¼ cup (2½ oz/75 g) Pear
Chutney (page 20)

About 6 oz (185 g) sliced
roasted turkey

2 oz (60 g) blue cheese,
crumbled

Mayonnaise

2 handfuls baby arugula

Preheat a panini maker according to the manufacturer's
instructions.

Brush 1 side of each bread slice with oil, then place the slices,
oiled side down, on a work surface. Spread the chutney on
2 of the bread slices, dividing it evenly. Arrange the turkey on
top of the chutney, dividing it evenly. Top the turkey with the
blue cheese. Spread the remaining 2 bread slices lightly with
mayonnaise and place them, mayonnaise side down, on top
of the blue cheese.

Place the sandwiches in the panini maker, close the top plate,
and cook until the bread is golden and toasted, the fillings
are warm, and the cheese is melted, 3–5 minutes.

Carefully open each sandwich, top with a handful of arugula,
and close the sandwich. Cut each sandwich in half and serve
right away.

Turkey Banh Mi

PREP TIME 10 MINUTES   **SERVES** 2

Two 6-inch (15-cm) baguette sections or 2 French rolls, about 6 inches (15 cm) long

Mayonnaise

Sriracha chili sauce

About 6 oz (185 g) sliced roasted turkey

¼ cup (1 oz/30 g) julienned pickled carrots

¼ cup (1 oz/30 g) julienned cucumber

Small handful fresh cilantro leaves

Split each baguette section horizontally. Spread the cut sides with mayonnaise and Sriracha sauce to taste. Arrange the turkey on the bottom halves, dividing it evenly. Top the turkey with the pickled carrots, cucumber, and cilantro, dividing them evenly. Close the sandwich with the top halves, mayonnaise side down.

Cut each sandwich in half, if desired, and serve right away.

Turkey with All the Trimmings Sandwich

PREP TIME 10 MINUTES   **SERVES** 2

4 slices coarse country bread

Olive oil

½ cup (5 oz/155 g) Port-Spiked Cranberry Sauce (page 74) or Cranberry-Orange Relish (page 76)

About 6 oz (185 g) sliced roasted turkey

½ cup (2 oz/60 g) stuffing

¼ cup (2 fl oz/60 ml) gravy, warmed

Brush 1 side of each bread slice with oil. Spread the cranberry sauce on the oiled sides, dividing evenly. Divide the turkey evenly between 2 slices of the bread. Top the turkey with the stuffing and gravy, dividing them evenly. Place the remaining bread slices on top, cranberry sauce side down.

Cut each sandwich in half and serve right away.

Menus

Creating a Thanksgiving menu that accommodates
the spirit of your celebration and the tastes of your guests
can be daunting. A good way to proceed is to select a
combination of dishes—one or two appetizers, a main,
some sides, and one or two desserts—that offers a variety
of colors, flavors, textures, and cooking times. You can opt
to serve a blend of traditional dishes and family favorites
mixed with new ideas from this book, or you can look
to this book to be your guide to the entire feast.
Here are six memorable menus to get you started.

MENU 1

Shrimp Bisque *(page 24)*

Classic Roasted Turkey *(page 29)*

Madeira-Sage Gravy *(page 72)*

Focaccia Stuffing with Chestnuts,
Bacon & Apples *(page 39)*

Candied Sweet Potatoes *(page 51)*

Mashed Potatoes with Herb-Infused Cream *(page 51)*

Green Bean Bundles with Bacon
& Brown Sugar *(page 55)*

Creamed Pearl Onions *(page 66)*

Everything Parker House Rolls *(page 45)*

Cranberry Compote with Riesling & Pears *(page 74)*

Desserts of your choice *(pages 81–89)*

MENU 2

Carrot Soup with Orange & Ginger *(page 25)*

Curry-Spiced Turkey *(page 29)*

Herbed Citrus Gravy *(page 73)*

Leek & Mushroom Stuffing *(page 42)*

Mashed Potatoes with Herb-Infused Cream *(page 51)*

Roasted Sweet Potatoes with Herbed Yogurt *(page 65)*

Gingered Winter Squash & Pear Purée *(page 58)*

Broccoli with Crisp Bread Crumbs *(page 59)*

Cranberry-Orange Relish *(page 76)*

Desserts of your choice *(pages 81–89)*

MENU 3

Arugula Salad with Goat Cheese & Pecans *(page 23)*

Cider-Brined, Spice-Rubbed Turkey *(page 30)*

Giblet Gravy *(page 72)*

Apple, Celery & Sourdough Stuffing *(page 43)*

Twice-Baked Sweet Potatoes *(page 52)*

Tangy Braised Greens *(page 55)*

Green Beans with Pecans *(page 56)*

Soufflé Spoon Bread with Cheddar Cheese *(page 46)*

Cranberry Compote with Riesling & Pears *(page 74)*

Desserts of your choice *(pages 81–89)*

MENU 4

Butternut Squash Soup *(page 24)*

Roasted Turkey with Herb Butter *(page 33)*

Port Gravy *(page 73)*

Oyster & Mushroom Stuffing *(page 42)*

Herbed Potato Gratin *(page 52)*

From-Scratch Green Bean Casserole *(page 56)*

Sautéed Mushrooms with Shallots & Sherry *(page 59)*

Honey-Roasted Spiced Carrots *(page 61)*

Cauliflower Steaks with Brown Butter *(page 66)*

Port-Spiked Cranberry Sauce *(page 74)*

Desserts of your choice *(pages 81–89)*

MENU 5

Mushroom Turnovers and
Crostini with Pear Chutney *(page 20)*

Spatchcocked Turkey with Herb Glaze *(page 33)*

Classic Turkey Gravy *(page 71)*

Spicy Corn Bread Stuffing with
Chorizo & Pepitas *(page 39)*

Candied Sweet Potatoes *(page 51)*

Brussels Sprouts & Butternut Squash
with Bacon *(page 58)*

Cheddar-Chive Biscuits *(page 47)*

Port-Spiked Cranberry Sauce *(page 74)*

Desserts of your choice *(pages 81–89)*

MENU 6

Watercress, Endive & Apple Salad *(page 23)*

Grill-Roasted Turkey with
Orange-Fennel Pan Gravy *(page 34)*

Corn Bread Stuffing with Apples,
Ham & Fennel *(page 40)*

Herbed Potato Gratin *(page 52)*

Brussels Sprouts with
Caramelized Shallots *(page 61)*

Wild Rice Pilaf with Butternut Squash
(page 62)

Sweet Potato Biscuits
with Honey Butter *(page 47)*

Cranberry-Orange Relish *(page 76)*

Desserts of your choice *(pages 81–89)*

Wine Pairings

Matching a single wine with all of the flavors that
make up a Thanksgiving feast can be challenging.
One good solution is to offer both a white and a red.
It is wise to include a few nonalcoholic options, too, such as
sparkling water or iced tea, allowing one quart or liter for
every two guests. Sparkling cider, hot spiced cider,
and cranberry lemonade are festive beverages that everyone
can enjoy. If you're looking for a more formal approach
to food and wine pairings, here are some suggestions:

○ Accompany appetizers and savory snacks with sparkling
wines, such as Champagne, Prosecco, or cava.

○ Match soup with a dry sherry, such as fino or Manzanilla.

○ Serve salads with a high-acid white, such as a Sauvignon
Blanc, or skip a wine altogether for the salad course. The
high acidity of many salad dressings can be difficult to
pair with wine.

○ Match turkey with crisp white wines, such as Sauvignon
Blanc, Spanish Albariño, or Italian Pinot Grigio, or with
a lightly oaked Chardonnay. Or, try a medium-bodied red,
such as Zinfandel, Syrah, or Pinot Noir.

○ Pair ham or other smoked foods with a fruity,
medium-bodied white or red wine, such as Riesling,
Gewürztraminer, Pinot Gris, or Pinot Noir.

○ Partner desserts with sweet wines that taste as sweet as
the dish, like vin santo or late-harvest whites and port
for chocolate desserts.

Turkey Know-How

Whether you're testing something new this year or using a tried-and-true family recipe, these pointers will help you serve your best turkey yet.

○ If you choose a frozen turkey, begin thawing it in the refrigerator well before you'll need to cook it. It will take about 4 hours per pound (500 g) to thaw completely.

○ If you choose a fresh turkey, order it at least a week in advance and pick it up the day before Thanksgiving.

○ Each of the stuffing recipes on pages 39–43 calls for baking the stuffing in a baking dish, which ensures the edges turn golden brown and deliciously crisp. An unstuffed turkey also roasts more evenly than a stuffed bird. If you prefer to roast the stuffing inside the turkey, follow these directions:

1. Line the turkey cavity with cheesecloth that's been folded in half, then fill the cavity with stuffing. This will make it easy to pull out all the stuffing once the turkey is cooked.

2. Be sure the stuffing is completely cool before packing it into the bird. Pack the stuffing loosely inside the turkey, as it will expand during cooking.

3. Add 30 minutes to the roasting time for birds up to 16 pounds (8 kg) and 1 hour for a larger turkey. Be sure the stuffing reaches at least 165°F (74°C) on an instant-read thermometer. (If it is not done when the bird is, transfer the stuffing to a buttered baking dish and continue to bake until done.)

4. Remove all of the stuffing from the cavity when the turkey is done and transfer it to a warmed dish. Do not let the stuffing sit for more than 2 hours in the turkey.

○ It is not necessary to truss a turkey, but trussing does create a more compact bird that is easier to carve. It is simple to do: Tuck the wing tips back under the turkey. Double a long piece of kitchen string. Bring the legs together and position the center of the string under the legs. Bring the ends of the string up and over the tops of the legs and cross the ends, making an X. Then, bring the ends back down under the legs, pulling the legs together tightly, and tie the string securely.

○ A spatchcocked turkey cooks quickly and evenly and all of the skin—not just the skin on the breast—turns a beautiful golden brown and crispy. Here are the directions to spatchcock a turkey:

1. Position the bird, breast side down, on a cutting board. Using kitchen shears or a large knife, cut along one side of the backbone until the bird is split open. Pull open the halves of the bird. Cut down the other side of the backbone to free it, then cut between the rib plates and remove any small pieces of bone.

2. Turn the bird, breast side up, opening it as flat as possible, and cover with a sheet of plastic wrap. Using your hands, press down firmly to break the breastbone and flatten the bird.

○ When basting, remove the roasting pan from the oven, close the oven door, and baste on the stove top. This will help keep your oven at the desired roasting temperature.

○ If the skin begins to brown too quickly, tent the turkey with aluminum foil.

○ Save all the browned bits and fat that collect in the bottom of the turkey roasting pan to make a homemade gravy. Follow the step-by-step instructions on page 103.

○ Carving a bird can seem daunting, but it is actually only a three-step process. Follow the instructions on page 104.

○ Garnish the turkey serving platter with fresh herb sprigs or bay leaves, small apples or citrus fruits, or wedges of pomegranate for a beautiful, natural presentation.

Gravy Primer

The prospect of making gravy intimidates some home cooks. But if you follow the steps below, you'll achieve a flavorful, lump-free gravy every time.

Step 1: Deglaze
Place the roasting pan with the pan drippings over 2 burners on the stove top. Pour the liquid of choice into the roasting pan and bring to a brisk simmer, scraping up the browned bits on the bottom of the pan.

Step 2: Degrease or strain
Pour the pan drippings into a fat separator, leaving the solids behind in the pan, and let stand for a few minutes. The fat will rise to the top. If you don't have a fat separator, pour the contents of the pan through a fine-mesh sieve set over a heatproof bowl; discard the solids in the sieve. Using a large spoon, skim off and discard the layer of fat that floats to the surface.

Step 3: Thicken the gravy
Follow the instructions in the recipe to make the gravy base, which usually involves mixing flour with a fat or cornstarch with a liquid. Pour the pan drippings into the gravy base, leaving the fat behind if using a fat separator, and simmer until thickened.

Carving Primer

The ritual of carving a whole roasted bird is a holiday mainstay. Follow the steps below and you'll impress everyone at the table with your carving prowess.

Step 1: Remove the legs

Place the turkey, breast side up, on the carving board. Using a carving knife, cut through the skin between a leg and the body. Gently pull the leg outward to locate the joint, then cut through the joint to remove the leg. Repeat with the second leg. Remove the wings in the same manner.

Step 2: Remove the breasts

Insert the fork along the side of the breast to steady the bird. Just above the thigh and wing joints, make a deep horizontal cut through the skin toward the bone. Make a thin cut along the breastbone, then using the tip of the knife, carefully carve downward along the bones and ribs of each side of the rib cage to remove each breast half.

Step 3: Slice and serve

To carve the drumsticks and thighs, cut between the joint to separate the drumstick and thigh. Secure the drumstick with the fork and slice the meat lengthwise along the bone, turning after each slice. Place the thigh, flat side down, and slice the meat parallel to the bone. Place the breast meat on the carving surface and cut crosswise into thin, uniform slices.

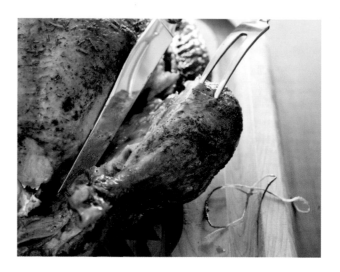

Chicken Stock

4 fresh flat-leaf parsley
stems

1 fresh thyme sprig

1 bay leaf

6 lb (3 kg) chicken parts,
such as backs, wings, necks,
and/or drumsticks

2 yellow onions, halved

2 leeks, white and light green
parts, cut into thirds

3 ribs celery, cut into thirds

3 carrots, cut into thirds

Tie the parsley, thyme, and bay leaf in a square of cheesecloth to
make a bouquet garni.

Combine the bouquet garni, chicken parts, onions, leeks, celery,
and carrots in a large stockpot. Add cold water just to cover
(about 3½ quarts/3.5 l). Slowly bring to a boil over medium heat,
then reduce the heat to low and simmer, uncovered, for 3 hours,
skimming off the foam.

Strain the stock through a sieve lined with cheesecloth into a
large bowl. If using right away, spoon off the visible fat or pour
into a fat separator. Otherwise, let cool for 1 hour, then cover and
refrigerate for at least 2 hours or for up to overnight. Using a large
spoon, remove the hardened fat from the surface and discard.

Refrigerate the stock in airtight containers for up to 3 days or
freeze for up to 3 months. Makes about 3 quarts (3 l).

Turkey Stock

Stems from 1 bunch fresh
flat-leaf parsley

2 fresh thyme sprigs

1 bay leaf

10 whole peppercorns

6 lb (3 kg) turkey parts, such
as wings, necks, and/or
drumsticks, wings halved at
the joint

1 yellow onion, quartered

1 turnip, quartered

3 ribs celery, cut into thirds

2 carrots, cut into thirds

Tie the parsley, thyme, bay leaf, and peppercorns in a square of
cheesecloth to make a bouquet garni.

Combine the bouquet garni, turkey parts, onion, turnip, celery,
and carrots in a large stockpot. Add cold water just to cover
(about 4 quarts/4 l). Slowly bring to a boil over medium heat,
then reduce the heat to low and simmer, uncovered, for 4 hours,
skimming off the foam.

Strain the stock through a sieve lined with cheesecloth into a
large bowl. If using right away, spoon off the visible fat or pour
into a fat separator. Otherwise, let cool for 1 hour, then cover and
refrigerate for at least 2 hours or for up to overnight. Using a large
spoon, remove the hardened fat from the surface and discard.

Refrigerate the stock in airtight containers for up to 3 days or
freeze for up to 3 months. Makes about 2½ quarts (2.5 l).

Vegetable Stock

2 yellow onions, thinly sliced

2 leeks, white and green
parts, sliced

4 ribs celery with leaves,
chopped

4 carrots, sliced lengthwise

1 red potato, diced

¼ lb (125 g) mushrooms,
brushed clean and quartered

6 cloves garlic

8 fresh flat-leaf parsley
stems

2 bay leaves

8 whole peppercorns

Combine all of the ingredients in a large stockpot. Add cold
water just to cover the ingredients (about 2½ quarts/2.5 l). Bring
to a boil over high heat, then reduce the heat to medium-low
and simmer, uncovered, for 1½ hours, skimming off the foam.

Let the stock cool slightly. Strain through a sieve lined with
cheesecloth into a large bowl. Press on the vegetables with the
back of a spoon to extract as much of the flavor as possible.
Let cool to room temperature. Refrigerate the stock in airtight
containers for up to 3 days or freeze for up to 3 months. Makes
about 8 cups (64 fl oz/2 l).

Basic Pie Dough

FOR A SINGLE-CRUST PIE
1¼ cups (6½ oz/200 g)
all-purpose flour

1 tablespoon sugar

1 teaspoon kosher salt

½ cup (4 oz/125 g) cold
unsalted butter, diced

3–4 tablespoons ice water

FOR A DOUBLE-CRUST PIE
2½ cups (12½ oz/390 g)
all-purpose flour

2 tablespoons sugar

2 teaspoons kosher salt

1 cup (8 oz/250 g) cold
unsalted butter, diced

6–8 tablespoons (3–4 fl oz/
90–125 ml) ice water

In a food processor, combine the flour, sugar, and salt and pulse to mix. Add the butter and pulse until the mixture resembles coarse meal, 10–15 pulses. Add the minimum amount of ice water and pulse twice. The dough should hold together when squeezed. If it is crumbly, add more water, 1 teaspoon at a time, pulsing twice after each addition.

Remove the dough from the food processor. Shape the dough into 1 disk for a single-crust pie, or into 2 disks for a double-crust pie. Wrap each dough disk in plastic wrap and refrigerate for at least 2 hours.

Preparing a Grill for Indirect-Heat Cooking

Gas grill

Preheat the grill using all of the burners, then turn off the burner(s) directly beneath where the food will sit. Place the food over the turned-off burner(s), and cover the grill.

Charcoal grill

When most of the coals are covered in a layer of gray ash, using a pair of long-handled tongs, arrange the coals in two equal piles on two opposite sides of the grate, leaving the center of the grate free of coals. Put the food on the center of the grill rack directly over the coal-free area and cover the grill.

Thanksgiving Equipment Checklist

Before you begin preparing your feast, it's a good idea to take an inventory of your tools and equipment to make sure that you have everything you will need on hand.

Essential Equipment

o Measuring cups and spoons

o Mixing bowls

o Knives and cutting boards

o Saucepans

o Sauté pans

o Frying pans

o Rimmed baking sheets

o Baking dishes

o Wooden spoons

o Blender

o Food processor

o Cheese grater

Turkey & Gravy Tools

o Instant-read thermometer

o Carving board

o Carving knife and fork

o Kitchen string

o Roasting pan and rack

o Basting brush

o Turkey lifters (optional)

o Brining container

o Whisk

o Fat separator (optional)

o Large metal spoon

o Fine-mesh sieve

Fruit & Vegetable Prep

o Vegetable peeler

o Garlic press

o Potato ricer

o Salad spinner

o Rasp grater

o Mandoline

o Colander

o Tongs

Baking Tools

o Stand mixer

o 9-inch (23-cm) pie pan or dish

o 9-inch (23-cm) deep-dish pie dish

o Pastry scraper

o Pastry brush

o Wire rack

o 9-inch (23-cm) springform pan

o Rolling pin

Index

weldonowen

1045 Sansome Street, Suite 100, San Francisco, CA 94111
www.weldonowen.com

THE BEST OF THANKSGIVING

Conceived and produced by Weldon Owen, Inc.
In collaboration with Williams-Sonoma, Inc.
3250 Van Ness Avenue, San Francisco, CA 94109

A WELDON OWEN PRODUCTION

Printed and bound in China by 1010 Printing, Ltd.

First printed in 2015
10 9 8 7 6 5 4 3 2 1

Library of Congress Cataloging-in-Publication
data is available.

ISBN 13: 978-1-61628-970-6
ISBN 10: 1-61628-970-8

Weldon Owen is a division of **BONNIER**

WELDON OWEN, INC

President & Publisher Roger Shaw
SVP, Sales & Marketing Amy Kaneko
Finance Manager Philip Paulick

Associate Publisher Amy Marr
Associate Editor Emma Rudolph

Creative Director Kelly Booth
Sr Production Designer Rachel Lopez Metzger

Production Director Chris Hemesath
Associate Production Director Michelle Duggan

Director of Enterprise Systems Shawn Macey
Imaging Manager Don Hill

ACKNOWLEDGMENTS
Weldon Owen wishes to thank the following people for their generous support
in producing this book: Kris Balloun, Peggy Fallon, Gloria Geller, Kim Laidlaw,
Monica S. Lee, Jennifer Newens, Elizabeth Parson, and Sharon Silva